31 TRAITS & QUALITIES OF HIGHLY SUCCESSFUL PEOPLE

LEARN THE ESSENTIAL TRAITS AND QUALITIES THAT TRANSFORM ORDINARY PEOPLE INTO EXTRAORDINARY ONES. CULTIVATING THESE TRAITS WITHIN YOURSELF CAN PAVE THE WAY FOR SUCCESS.

MOHAMMAD AKBAR

Made with ♥ on the Notion Press Platform
www.notionpress.com

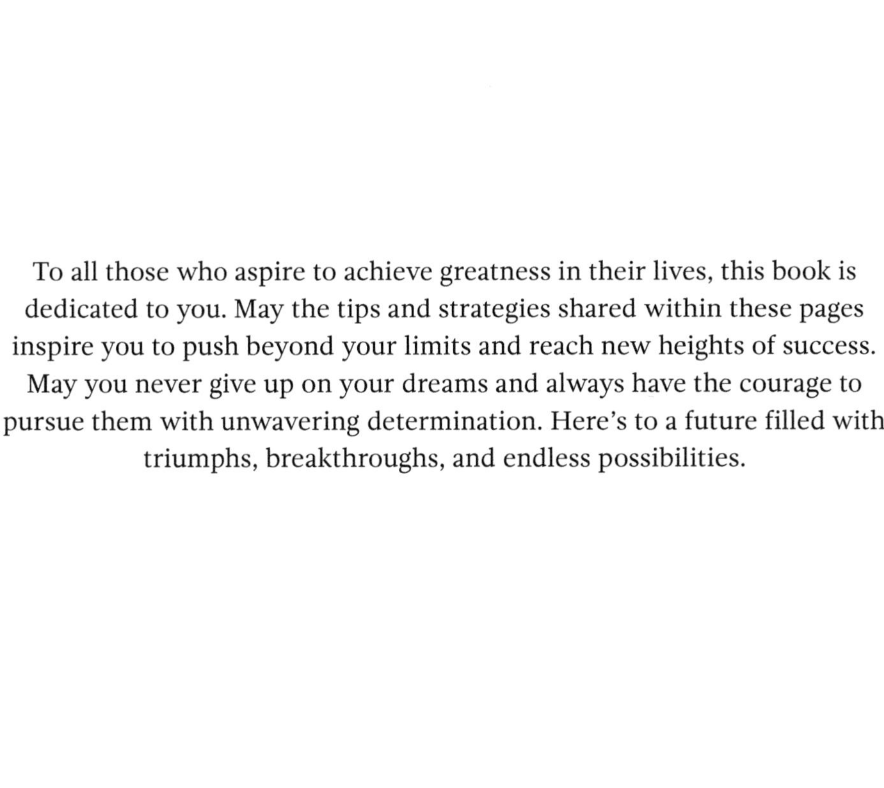

To all those who aspire to achieve greatness in their lives, this book is dedicated to you. May the tips and strategies shared within these pages inspire you to push beyond your limits and reach new heights of success. May you never give up on your dreams and always have the courage to pursue them with unwavering determination. Here's to a future filled with triumphs, breakthroughs, and endless possibilities.

Contents

Contents

Foreword

Success is a subject that has fascinated humans for centuries. We are always searching for the secret formula that leads to achieving our dreams and accomplishing our goals. However, the truth is that success is not just about luck or talent. It requires a set of qualities and traits that highly successful people possess.

Success is a journey, not a destination. It requires patience, perseverance, and a willingness to learn from our successes and failures. This understanding forms the core of the book you are about to read.

This book will explore the essential qualities and traits of highly successful people. Drawing from the experiences of successful individuals across various fields, we will delve into the key habits, mindsets, and behaviors that have propelled them to the top of their respective industries.

Whether you are an aspiring entrepreneur, a student looking to excel academically, or anyone seeking success in any area of life, this book will provide invaluable insights and practical tips to apply to your journey.

I am confident that by the end of this book, you will understand what it takes to become highly successful and be inspired to take action toward achieving your goals. So, let's begin this journey together and learn from the best of the best.

Preface

Success means different things to different people. For some, it's about achieving financial stability or career recognition. For others, it's about fulfilling personal goals or positively impacting the world around them. Regardless of what success means to you, one thing is certain: it requires effort, dedication, and a willingness to learn.

The purpose of this book is to provide you with practical tips and strategies that you can apply to your own life, regardless of your definition of success. The insights shared within these pages are not theoretical or abstract; they are based on the experiences and lessons learned from successful individuals across various fields.

Each chapter covers a different aspect of success, from goal setting and time management to communication and leadership. While each chapter can be read independently, they are all interconnected and build upon each other to provide a comprehensive guide to achieving success.

It's important to note that the tips and strategies presented in this book do not guarantee success. Success is not a one-size-fits-all concept; what works for one person may not work for another. However, by incorporating these tips into your own life, you will be better equipped to navigate the challenges of pursuing your goals.

I hope this book is a valuable resource for you on your journey toward success. May the insights shared within these pages inspire, motivate, and guide you toward achieving your definition of success.

Acknowledgements

Writing a book is never a solitary effort. It takes many individuals' support, encouragement, and expertise to bring a project like this to fruition. I want to express my heartfelt gratitude to everyone, especially my wife, who contributed to the creation of this book.

First and foremost, I want to thank the successful individuals who generously shared their experiences and insights with me. Your wisdom and advice are invaluable, and I am honored to have had the opportunity to learn from you.

My friends and family, thank you for your unwavering support and encouragement. Your belief in me and this project motivated me to keep pushing forward, even when the going got tough.

Finally, I would like to thank my readers, who have taken the time to engage with this book. I hope the tips and strategies shared within these pages will help you on your journey toward success. Thank you for allowing me to be a part of that journey.

Without the support of all these individuals, this book would not have been possible. I am deeply grateful for every one of you.

Prologue

What makes highly successful people stand out from the rest of us? Is it their intelligence, their charisma, or their talents? While these factors certainly play a role, they do not fully explain why some individuals achieve extraordinary success while others struggle to make ends meet.

The truth is that highly successful people possess unique qualities and traits that enable them to thrive in any environment. They have a way of thinking, acting, and communicating that sets them apart from the crowd and allows them to achieve their goals.

Success is a journey that requires hard work, perseverance, and a willingness to learn. It's a journey that can be both exhilarating and daunting, filled with ups and downs, triumphs and setbacks.

In this book, we will explore these qualities and traits in detail. We will look at the habits and routines that highly successful people follow, the mindsets they adopt, and the skills they have honed over years of practice.

The journey toward success is not always easy, but it is always worth it. It's a journey that requires courage, determination, and a willingness to learn from successes and failures. This book is a valuable resource for you on your journey toward success. May the insights shared within these pages inspire, motivate, and guide you toward achieving your definition of success.

CHAPTER ONE

AMBITION

Ambition is crucial to success as it provides the drive, motivation, and determination to overcome obstacles and achieve one's goals. Without ambition, it isn't easy to maintain the focus and perseverance required to succeed.

What Is Ambition?

Ambition is a powerful driving force that motivates individuals to pursue their goals and dreams. It is a quality that enables people to aim high and strive toward achieving success and fulfillment in life. Ambition can be described as a strong desire and determination to achieve something often considered challenging.

Ambition is not limited to any particular area of life; it can apply to careers, relationships, personal growth, or any other aspect of life. Ambitious individuals are driven by a desire to excel and make a difference in the world. They set goals for themselves and work tirelessly to achieve them, often overcoming obstacles and challenges.

The nature of ambition can vary significantly from person to person. Some people have an innate sense of ambition, while others develop it over time through their life experiences. Ambition can also take on different forms, ranging from a desire for financial success to pursuing artistic or intellectual excellence.

While ambition can be a powerful force for achieving success, it can also have adverse effects if not balanced with other aspects of life. Overly ambitious individuals may neglect their personal relationships or health to pursue their goals, leading to burnout and other negative consequences. Maintaining a healthy balance between ambition and other important aspects of life is important.

In conclusion, ambition is a robust quality that drives individuals to pursue their goals and dreams. It can lead to outstanding achievements and personal fulfillment, but it must be balanced with other aspects of life to avoid negative consequences. Ambition is essential to success, but it is important to remember that success is not the only measure of a fulfilling life.

Why Is Ambition Important?

Ambition is an important trait that can help individuals achieve success and fulfillment in life. It provides the drive and motivation needed to set and pursue goals, overcome obstacles, and accomplish great things.

Here are a few reasons why ambition is important:

Drives Personal Growth

Ambition encourages individuals to strive for improvement and growth continuously. By setting ambitious goals and working towards achieving them, individuals are forced to step outside their comfort zones, learn new skills, and develop new strengths. It, in turn, can lead to personal growth and development.

Fuels Achievement

Ambition is often the driving force behind great achievements. Without ambition, individuals may lack the motivation and perseverance needed to accomplish their goals. By setting high standards and working hard to achieve them, ambitious individuals can accomplish great things and make a significant impact in their chosen fields.

Enhances Self-Esteem

Achieving ambitious goals can boost self-esteem and confidence. When individuals set and achieve challenging goals, they gain a sense of accomplishment and pride in their abilities. It can lead to increased confidence and a more positive self-image.

Fosters Creativity and Innovation

Ambition can drive individuals to think outside the box and develop new and innovative solutions to problems. By setting ambitious goals and striving for excellence, individuals may be more likely to take risks and try new things, leading to creativity and innovation.

Creates Opportunities

Ambition can open doors and create opportunities for individuals. By setting ambitious goals and working hard to achieve them, individuals may gain recognition and respect within their fields, leading to new opportunities for advancement and success.

Inspires Others

Ambitious individuals can be role models and inspire others to pursue their goals and dreams. By setting an example of hard work and determination, ambitious individuals can motivate and inspire others to do the same.

In conclusion, ambition is an important trait that can lead to personal growth, achievement, self-esteem, creativity, opportunity, and inspiration. While ambition can be a powerful force for good, it is important to balance it with other aspects of life and avoid becoming overly fixated on success.

With the right mindset and approach, ambition can be a powerful tool for achieving success and fulfillment in life.

How to Be More Ambitious?

Being ambitious means having a strong desire to achieve something often considered challenging. Ambition can help individuals achieve success and fulfillment in life.

If you're looking to be more ambitious, here are some tips to get started:

Define Your Goals

The first step to being more ambitious is to define your goals. What do you want to achieve? Be specific about your goals and make sure they are realistic and attainable. Write them down and keep them somewhere visible to remind you of what you're working towards.

Create A Plan

Once you've defined your goals, create a plan to achieve them. Break down your goals into smaller, more manageable tasks and set deadlines for each. Having a plan in place can help you stay focused and motivated.

Take Action

It's not enough to have goals and a plan. It would help if you took action to make them a reality. Start working towards your goals today, even if it's just a small step. Consistent effort over time can lead to significant progress.

Embrace Failure

Failure is a natural part of the process when working towards ambitious goals. Don't be afraid to fail; don't let failure discourage you. Instead, learn from your mistakes and use them as opportunities for growth and improvement.

Seek Feedback

Getting feedback from others can be a valuable tool for achieving ambitious goals. Ask for feedback from mentors, colleagues, or friends with experience in your field. Use their feedback to improve and refine your approach.

Expand Your Network

Building a strong network of contacts can help you achieve your goals. Attend networking events, join professional organizations, and connect with others in your field. Building relationships with others can lead to new opportunities and collaborations.

Stay Focused

It's easy to get distracted and lose sight of your goals. Stay focused and remind yourself why you're working towards your objectives. Use visualization techniques to imagine yourself achieving your goals and experiencing the benefits of success.

Take Risks

Being ambitious often involves taking risks. Don't be afraid to take calculated risks and step outside your comfort zone. Sometimes the most significant rewards come from taking bold action.

Keep Learning

Continuously learning and growing is essential for achieving ambitious goals. Seek new knowledge, take classes or workshops, and stay current with industry trends. You can become more effective and successful by continually expanding your knowledge and skills.

Celebrate Your Successes

Finally, don't forget to celebrate your successes along the way. Recognize and acknowledge your accomplishments, no matter how small they may seem. Celebrating your successes can help you stay motivated and inspire you to keep pushing toward your goals.

In conclusion, being ambitious can help individuals achieve great things in life. By defining your goals, creating a plan, taking action, embracing failure, seeking feedback, expanding your network, staying focused, taking risks, learning continuously, and celebrating your successes, you can be more ambitious and achieve your goals. Remember that ambition is a journey, not a destination, and that working towards ambitious goals can be just as rewarding as the end result.

Examples Of Ambition In Life

Setting an ambition is essential to achieving success in any aspect of life. Ambition gives individuals a sense of purpose and direction, motivating them to work hard and persevere through challenges. Identifying what you want to achieve and why it's important is crucial. It could involve setting specific goals and outlining the steps needed to achieve them.

When setting an ambition, it's also important to consider your strengths and weaknesses and any external factors that may impact your progress. Setting realistic and achievable goals is important, as this will help you stay motivated and avoid feeling discouraged.

Additionally, it's important to have a plan in place for achieving your ambition. It could involve breaking down your goals into smaller, more manageable tasks and setting deadlines for each one. Having a plan, you can stay focused and on track, even when faced with obstacles or setbacks.

Overall, setting an ambition is a critical step towards achieving success in any area of life. By identifying your goals, creating a plan, and staying focused and motivated, you can progress toward achieving your ambitions and creating a fulfilling and rewarding life.

As we've learned that setting an ambition is very important in life. Let's see the ten examples of ambition in life:

Starting A Business

Many entrepreneurs have ambitious goals of starting their businesses and becoming successful. It requires hard work, dedication, and risk-taking, but the rewards can be significant.

Pursuing Higher Education

Many aspire to pursue higher education to further their careers and expand their knowledge. It can involve obtaining advanced degrees or taking specialized courses.

Achieving Financial Independence

Ambitious individuals may have goals of achieving financial independence, whether through investing, saving, or building a successful career.

Climbing The Corporate Ladder

Some people have ambitious goals of climbing the corporate ladder and becoming top executives in their companies. It requires a lot of hard work, dedication, and strategic planning.

Becoming An Expert In A Field

Ambitious individuals may desire to become experts in their field, whether it's a specific industry, skillset, or subject matter.

Pursuing Creative Endeavours

Many individuals have ambitious goals of pursuing creative endeavors, such as writing a novel, making a film, or creating a piece of art. It can require a lot of dedication and hard work, but the rewards can be significant.

Making A Positive Impact In The World

Ambitious individuals may have goals of making a positive impact in the world, whether it's through philanthropy, activism, or social entrepreneurship.

Achieving Physical Fitness

Many people aim to achieve physical fitness and become their healthiest selves. It can involve working with personal trainers, following strict diets, and dedicating time to exercise.

Traveling The World

Ambitious individuals may have goals of traveling the world, experiencing different cultures, and seeing new sights. It can require a lot of planning and dedication, but the rewards can be life-changing.

Overcoming Personal Challenges

Many individuals have ambitious goals of overcoming personal challenges, whether overcoming addiction, healing from trauma, or improving their mental health. It requires a lot of courage and hard work, but the rewards can be immeasurable.

CHAPTER TWO

POSITIVE ATTITUDE

A positive attitude plays a critical role in success as it helps individuals stay focused, motivated, and resilient in facing challenges. It also attracts positivity and opportunities, leading to a more fulfilling and successful life.

What Is a Positive Attitude?

A positive attitude is a mindset that focuses on the good in life and approaches challenges with an optimistic outlook. It is characterized by hopefulness, gratitude, and a willingness to embrace change and growth. A positive attitude can have numerous benefits, including improved mental and physical health, increased productivity, and greater resilience in adversity.

Having a positive attitude means looking for the silver lining in every situation, no matter how challenging it may be. It involves reframing negative thoughts into positive ones and focusing on solutions rather than problems. It also means being open-minded and willing to learn from experiences, even when they are uncomfortable or unpleasant.

People with a positive attitude tend to be more resilient and adaptable in the face of change, as they can see challenges as opportunities for growth and improvement. They are also more likely to build strong relationships and foster community, as they can approach others with kindness and empathy.

Cultivating a positive attitude takes practice and intentionality. Some strategies for developing a more positive outlook include practicing gratitude, setting realistic goals, focusing on solutions rather than problems, and surrounding oneself with positive and supportive people. Taking care of oneself by engaging in regular self-care activities such as exercise, meditation, or spending time in nature is also important.

Ultimately, a positive attitude is a choice that we can make each day. By focusing on the good in life and approaching challenges with optimism, we can build a sense of resilience and joy that can sustain us through even the most challenging times.

How to Develop Positive Attitude?

Developing a positive attitude is a process that takes time and effort, but it can be one of the most rewarding things you can do for yourself. It involves a conscious effort to focus on the positive aspects of your life, challenge negative thoughts, and cultivate a mindset of gratitude and optimism. It can include things like practicing self-care, surrounding yourself with positive people, and learning from mistakes.

By making small changes and consistently developing a positive attitude, you can improve your mental and physical health, build stronger relationships, and increase your chances of success in all areas of your life. Remember that developing a positive attitude is a journey, and it's important to be patient and kind to yourself as you work toward this goal.

Tips To Develop Positive Attitude

Practice Gratitude

Take time each day to reflect on the things you are thankful for in your life. It can help shift your focus to the positive aspects of your life.

Challenge Negative Thoughts

Notice when negative thoughts arise and challenge them with positive ones. It can help you reframe your perspective and see things more positively.

Surround Yourself with Positive People

Spend time with people who have a positive attitude. Being around positive energy can help boost your positivity.

Practice Self-Care

Take care of your physical, mental, and emotional health by engaging in activities that make you feel good, such as exercise, meditation, or spending time in nature.

Focus on Solutions

When faced with challenges or problems, focus on finding solutions rather than dwelling on the negative aspects of the situation.

Cultivate Optimism

Practice looking on the bright side and finding the silver lining in every situation.

Learn from Mistakes

View mistakes as opportunities for growth and learning. It can help you approach challenges with a positive attitude.

Set Realistic Goals

Set achievable goals for yourself and celebrate your progress along the way.

Laugh More

Find humor in everyday situations and allow yourself to laugh and have fun.

Practice Mindfulness

Be present at the moment and focus on the here and now. It can help reduce stress and increase feelings of positivity.

Why is a Positive Attitude Important?

Developing a positive attitude is important for a variety of reasons. It can improve mental and physical health, increase resilience in the face of challenges, and enhance overall well-being.

Here are a few reasons why developing a positive attitude is so important:

Better Mental Health

Studies have shown that having a positive attitude can improve mental health by reducing symptoms of depression and anxiety. It can also help reduce stress and increase feelings of happiness and well-being.

Improved Physical Health

A positive attitude can also have physical health benefits, such as lowering blood pressure and reducing the risk of heart disease. It can also help boost the immune system and increase longevity.

Increased Resilience

A positive attitude can help build resilience in facing challenges and setbacks. It can help you approach difficult situations with optimism and problem-solving skills.

Enhanced Relationships

A positive attitude can help you build stronger relationships with others. It can help you approach others with kindness and empathy and make you more approachable and likable.

Greater Success

People with positive attitudes tend to be more successful personally and professionally. They are often more motivated and productive and generally have a better outlook on life.

Overall, developing a positive attitude can have numerous benefits that can enhance all areas of your life. Focusing on the positive can improve your mental and physical health, build stronger relationships, and increase your chances of success.

How Do You Show a Positive Attitude in the Workplace?

Showing a positive workplace attitude is important for personal and professional growth. A positive attitude can lead to better colleague relationships, increased productivity, and improved job satisfaction.

Here are some ways to show a positive attitude in the workplace:

Greet Others With A Smile

A smile can go a long way in showing others that you are approachable and friendly. It can also help to create a positive atmosphere in the workplace.

Be Respectful

Showing respect to colleagues, regardless of their position, is important to maintaining a positive workplace environment. It can involve things like listening attentively when someone is speaking, avoiding gossip, and being mindful of others‘ time.

Communicate Effectively

Effective communication is key to maintaining positive relationships in the workplace. It can involve speaking clearly and concisely, actively listening to others, and using positive language.

Show Appreciation

Expressing gratitude and appreciation for colleagues' work can help to foster a positive workplace culture. It can involve thanking someone for their help, acknowledging a job well done, or simply expressing gratitude for being part of a supportive team.

Be Adaptable

Being adaptable and open to change can help to create a positive work environment. It can involve being flexible in your approach to work, being willing to learn new skills, and embracing new ideas and perspectives.

Offer Solutions

When faced with a problem, offering solutions rather than focusing on the negative aspects can help maintain a positive workplace attitude. It can involve brainstorming with colleagues, offering constructive feedback, and seeking creative solutions.

Take Care Of Yourself

Taking care of your physical, mental, and emotional health is an important part of maintaining a positive attitude in the workplace. It can involve taking regular breaks, practicing self-care, and seeking support when needed.

Overall, showing a positive attitude in the workplace is important for maintaining healthy relationships with colleagues, increasing productivity, and fostering a positive workplace culture. By being respectful, communicating effectively, showing appreciation, being adaptable, offering solutions, and taking care of yourself, you can help to create a positive work environment where everyone feels valued and supported.

CHAPTER THREE

SELF- CONFIDENCE

Self-confidence plays a crucial role in success as it allows individuals to believe in their abilities and take risks, persevere through obstacles, and maintain a positive attitude in the face of adversity. Individuals may hold themselves back from reaching their full potential and pursuing their goals without self-confidence.

What Is Self-Confidence?

Self-confidence is the belief in one's abilities, qualities, and judgments. It is the trust one has in oneself to handle situations, overcome obstacles, and achieve goals. Self-confidence is essential to human development, enabling individuals to take risks, make decisions, and pursue their dreams.

Self-confidence is often developed over time through experiences, learning, and personal growth. When individuals face challenges and overcome them successfully, they become more confident in handling future obstacles. Similarly, when individuals learn new skills or gain knowledge, they become more confident in applying these skills to achieve their goals.

Self-confidence is crucial in various aspects of life, such as personal relationships, academic or professional success, and mental and emotional well-being. Individuals with high levels of self-confidence tend to be more assertive, have better communication skills, and form healthier relationships. Self-confident individuals are more likely to take on leadership roles, speak up in meetings, and pursue career advancements in the workplace.

On the other hand, low self-confidence can negatively impact an individual's life. People with low self-confidence may doubt their abilities, shy away from challenges, and avoid taking risks, which can hinder their personal and professional growth. Low self-confidence can also lead to anxiety, stress, and other mental health issues.

Self-confidence can be improved through various methods, such as positive self-talk, visualization, setting and achieving goals, and seeking support from others. Individuals can boost their self-confidence and develop a more positive self-image by practicing self-compassion, celebrating small achievements, and reframing negative self-talk.

In conclusion, self-confidence is believing in oneself to handle challenges, achieve goals, and make decisions. It is a vital aspect of personal and professional development and impacts an individual's mental and emotional well-being. Individuals can improve their relationships, career prospects, and overall quality of life by developing and nurturing self-confidence.

How Does Self-Confidence Lead to Success?

Self-confidence is a crucial factor that contributes to success. People with high levels of self-confidence tend to perform better, take on challenges, and achieve their goals more effectively. It is because self-confidence gives individuals the necessary mindset and attitude to succeed.

One way in which self-confidence leads to success is by enabling individuals to take risks. People with high levels of self-confidence are more willing to take on new challenges and pursue their goals, even if they are uncertain about the outcome. They believe in their abilities to handle any situation and are not afraid of failure. As a result, they are more likely to take risks that can lead to success.

Self-confidence also enables individuals to maintain a positive attitude and mindset. People with self-confidence tend to focus on their strengths and abilities rather than their weaknesses and limitations. They have a "can-do" attitude and believe they can achieve anything they set their minds to. This positive attitude helps them overcome obstacles and challenges and keep moving toward their goals.

Moreover, self-confidence helps individuals to perform better. People who believe in their abilities tend to work harder and be more productive. They are not afraid to take on challenging tasks and are likelier to put in the effort required to achieve their goals. The increased productivity and focus can lead to success in various areas of life, including personal relationships, academic or professional pursuits, and sports.

Finally, self-confidence can help individuals create a positive image of themselves, leading to success in various social and professional settings. People with self-confidence tend to be more assertive, have better communication skills, and form healthier relationships. Self-confident individuals are more likely to take on leadership roles, speak up in meetings, and pursue career advancements in the workplace.

In conclusion, self-confidence is a crucial factor that contributes to success. It enables individuals to take risks, maintain a positive attitude, perform better, and create a positive image of themselves. By developing and nurturing self-confidence, individuals can improve their chances of success in various areas of life.

How to Develop Self-Confidence?

Self-confidence is an essential aspect of personal and professional development. It is the belief in oneself to handle challenges, achieve goals, and make decisions. Developing self-confidence is a process that requires patience, practice, and dedication.

Here are some practical steps to help you develop self-confidence:

Identify Your Strengths

Start by identifying your strengths and areas of expertise. Make a list of your achievements, talents, and skills. Focusing on your strengths can boost your confidence and create a positive self-image.

Set Realistic Goals

Setting achievable goals can help you build self-confidence. Break down your goals into smaller, manageable steps and celebrate each milestone you achieve. You can build momentum and confidence to tackle more significant challenges by achieving small goals.

Face Your Fears

Facing your fears is an effective way to boost self-confidence. Start by identifying the things that scare you and take small steps to overcome them. Gradually expose yourself to your fears, and celebrate each success along the way. By facing your fears, you can build resilience and confidence in your ability to handle challenges.

Practice Self-Care

Taking care of yourself can help boost your confidence. Practice good self-care habits, such as eating healthy foods, getting enough sleep, and engaging in regular physical activity. These habits can help you feel better about yourself and boost your self-image.

Surround Yourself With Positive People

Surrounding yourself with positive and supportive people can help boost your confidence. Seek out people who encourage and support you, and avoid those who bring you down. Positive people can help you feel better about yourself and build your confidence.

Visualize Success

Visualization is a powerful technique that can help boost self-confidence. Close your eyes and visualize yourself succeeding in a particular task or situation. Imagine yourself handling challenges with ease and achieving your goals. Visualization can help you build confidence in your ability to succeed.

Practice Self-Compassion

Self-compassion is essential in developing self-confidence. Be kind to yourself and avoid negative self-talk. Celebrate your successes, no matter how small, and be gentle with yourself when you make mistakes. By practicing self-compassion, you can build a positive self-image and boost self-confidence.

Learn From Failure

Failure is a natural part of life and can be an opportunity for growth. When you experience failure, take the time to reflect on what went wrong and what you can learn from the experience. Use the lessons learned to improve your skills and abilities, and try again. Learning from failure can help you build resilience and confidence in your ability to handle challenges.

Take On New Challenges

Taking on new challenges can help you build self-confidence. Step outside of your comfort zone and try something new. Challenge yourself to learn a new skill, take on a leadership role, or pursue a new hobby. By taking on new challenges, you can build confidence in your ability to handle new situations.

Practice Gratitude

Gratitude is a powerful tool that can help boost self-confidence. Take the time to reflect on what you are grateful for in your life, and focus on the positive aspects of your experiences. By practicing gratitude, you can build a positive outlook on life and boost your self-confidence.

In conclusion, developing self-confidence is a process that requires patience, practice, and dedication. By identifying your strengths, setting realistic goals, facing your fears, practicing self-care, surrounding yourself with positive people, visualizing success, practicing self-compassion, learning from failure, taking on new challenges, and practicing gratitude, you can build self-confidence and achieving your goals.

Importance of Self-Confidence in the Workplace

Self-confidence is a crucial factor in achieving success in the workplace. It is the belief in oneself to handle challenges, make decisions, and achieve goals. Self-confidence can lead to better job performance, improved relationships with colleagues and managers, and a more positive work environment.

Here are some reasons why self-confidence is important in the workplace:

Better Job Performance

People with self-confidence tend to perform better in their jobs. They are more willing to take on challenging tasks, work harder, and take risks. Self-confidence gives individuals a "can-do" attitude, leading to increased productivity and better job performance.

Improved Relationships

Self-confidence can improve relationships with colleagues and managers. People with self-confidence tend to communicate more effectively, be more assertive, and form healthier relationships. They are more likely to speak up in meetings, express their ideas, and contribute to the team.

Increased Job Satisfaction

Self-confidence can lead to increased job satisfaction. People with self-confidence tend to feel more fulfilled in their work, as they are more likely to achieve their goals and feel good about their contributions. It can lead to a more positive work environment and increased morale.

Better Leadership Skills

Self-confidence is essential in leadership positions. Self-confident leaders are more likely to inspire and motivate their team, make tough decisions, and easily handle challenges. Self-confidence enables leaders to have a clear vision and direction for their team, which can lead to improved performance and success.

Improved Career Prospects

Self-confidence can improve career prospects. People with self-confidence are more likely to pursue career advancements, take on leadership roles, and pursue new opportunities. Self-confidence enables individuals to take risks and seize opportunities, which can lead to career growth and success.

Reduced Stress

Self-confidence can reduce stress in the workplace. People with self-confidence tend to feel more in control of their work and environment, which can reduce stress levels. It can lead to a more positive work environment, improved colleague relationships, and better job performance.

In conclusion, self-confidence is a crucial factor in achieving success in the workplace. It can lead to better job performance, improved relationships with colleagues and managers, increased job satisfaction, better leadership skills, improved career prospects, and reduced stress. By developing and nurturing self-confidence, individuals can improve their chances of success in the workplace and achieve their career goals.

CHAPTER FOUR

TIME MANAGEMENT

Time management is a critical skill for success as it allows individuals to prioritize tasks, focus on high-value activities, and make the most of their available time, leading to greater productivity, efficiency, and achievement of goals. Without effective time management, individuals may struggle to stay organized, meet deadlines, and maximize their potential.

What Is Time Management?

Time management is using your time efficiently to achieve your goals and objectives. It involves prioritizing tasks, planning and scheduling activities, and setting goals and deadlines to ensure that you make the most of your time.

Effective time management skills are crucial in today's fast-paced world, where we are constantly bombarded with numerous distractions and demands on our time. Without proper time management, we can easily get overwhelmed and struggle to keep up with our responsibilities.

Time management begins with setting goals and objectives. It involves identifying your goals and setting realistic deadlines for each task. Once you have a clear idea of your goals, you can prioritize your tasks based on their importance and urgency.

One effective way to manage your time is to create a to-do list. It involves listing all the tasks you need to complete and organizing them in order of importance. You can then allocate time to each task based on their priority level and work on them accordingly.

Another effective time management technique is to use a calendar or planner. It involves scheduling your tasks and activities in advance so you know exactly what you need to do and when. It can help you stay focused and avoid procrastination.

Effective time management also requires self-discipline and the ability to say no to distractions and interruptions. It means avoiding time-wasting activities such as social media, email, and other distractions that can take up valuable time.

In summary, time management is an essential skill for anyone who wants to achieve their goals and be successful in their personal and professional lives. By prioritizing tasks, setting goals and deadlines, and avoiding distractions, you can make the most of your time and achieve your objectives efficiently and effectively.

Why Is Time Management Important?

Time management is important because it enables you to make the most of your time, which is a finite resource. Effective time management allows you to accomplish more in less time, reduce stress and anxiety, improve your productivity, and achieve your goals more efficiently.

Here are some reasons why time management is important:

Increased Productivity

Effective time management lets you prioritize your tasks and work on the most important ones first. It helps you accomplish more in less time, resulting in increased productivity.

Less Stress and Anxiety

Poor time management can lead to stress and anxiety as you struggle to keep up with your responsibilities. Effective time management, on the other hand, helps you stay organized and focused, reducing stress and anxiety.

Improved Quality of Work

When you manage your time effectively, you can devote more time and attention to each task, resulting in higher-quality work.

Better Work-Life Balance

Effective time management can help you balance your work and personal life by enabling you to prioritize your tasks and make time for the things that matter most to you.

Greater Opportunities

Effective time management allows you to accomplish more in less time, opening up more significant opportunities for personal and professional growth.

Improved Decision-Making

When you manage your time effectively, you can make better decisions because you clearly understand your priorities and goals.

Increased Accountability

Effective time management helps you stay accountable to yourself and others by enabling you to set clear goals and deadlines and track your progress toward them.

In conclusion, time management is important because it helps you accomplish more in less time, reduces stress and anxiety, improves your productivity and the quality of your work, and enables you to achieve your goals more efficiently. By learning and implementing effective time management strategies, you can make the most of your time and succeed in all areas of your life.

What Are Time Management Techniques?

Effective time management techniques are essential for anyone looking to achieve their goals and increase productivity. Here are some of the best time management techniques that can help you manage your time more effectively:

Prioritize Your Tasks

One of the most effective time management techniques is prioritizing your tasks based on their importance and urgency. You can use tools like Eisenhower Matrix, ABC analysis, or simply a to-do list to categorize tasks based on their priority level.

The idea is to focus on important and urgent tasks first, followed by important but not urgent ones. Then, you can work on tasks that are urgent but not important, and finally, tasks that are neither important nor urgent.

Use Time-Blocking

Time-blocking is a technique that involves scheduling your tasks and activities in specific time slots throughout the day. It helps you stay organized and focused on one task at a time, avoiding multitasking and distractions.

To use time-blocking, identify the tasks you need to complete and estimate how long each task will take. Then, create a schedule that blocks out specific time slots for each task, allocating more time to significant and complex tasks.

Practice The Pomodoro Technique

The Pomodoro Technique is a time management technique that involves breaking your work into short, focused intervals called Pomodoros. Each Pomodoro is typically 25 minutes long, followed by a 5-minute break.

The idea is to work on one task for the entire Pomodoro, avoiding distractions and interruptions. After each Pomodoro, take a short break to recharge before starting the next one.

Eliminate Distractions

Distractions can waste a lot of time and reduce your productivity. You must eliminate distractions as much as possible to manage your time effectively.

Some practical ways to eliminate distractions include turning off notifications on your phone and computer, closing unnecessary tabs on your browser, and working in a quiet and focused environment.

Take Regular Breaks

Taking regular breaks is essential for managing your time effectively. It may seem counterintuitive, but taking breaks can improve productivity by helping you recharge and refocus.

Try to take short breaks every hour or so, and take longer breaks after completing a task or milestone. Use this time to stretch, walk, or do something that helps you relax and recharge.

Learn to Say No

Learning to say no is a critical time management technique to help you avoid overcommitting and feeling overwhelmed. It's okay to say no to requests that don't align with your goals or priorities.

When someone asks you to do something, consider whether it aligns with your goals and whether you have the time and resources to complete it effectively. If not, don't be afraid to say no.

Use Technology to Your Advantage

Technology can be a powerful tool for managing your time effectively. Many apps and tools can help you stay organized, manage your schedule, and automate repetitive tasks.

In conclusion, effective time management is essential for achieving your goals and increasing your productivity. By prioritizing your tasks, eliminating distractions, taking regular breaks, learning to say no, and using technology to your advantage, you can manage your time more effectively and succeed in all areas of your life.

Time Management in the Workplace

Effective time management is crucial for workplace productivity and individual employees, and the organization. Implementing time management strategies in the workplace can lead to increased productivity, improved job satisfaction, and a better work-life balance.

Here are some tips for implementing time management in the workplace:

Set Clear Goals and Priorities

Setting clear goals and priorities is essential for effective time management in the workplace. It involves defining specific objectives for each employee or team and prioritizing tasks based on their importance and urgency.

By setting clear goals and priorities, employees can focus on the most important tasks, avoid wasting time on unimportant tasks, and ensure they work towards the organization's overall objectives.

Create a Schedule and Stick to It

Creating a schedule is essential to effective time management in the workplace. It involves setting specific times for tasks, meetings, and other activities and sticking to the schedule as much as possible.

It can help employees stay organized and focused, avoid multitasking, and ensure that they have enough time to complete their work. It also helps to reduce stress and improve job satisfaction by providing structure and predictability to the workday.

Use Time Management Tools and Techniques

Employees can use many time management tools and techniques to manage their time effectively. For example, time-blocking, Pomodoro Technique, and prioritization tools can help employees prioritize their tasks, manage their schedule, and avoid distractions.

Organizations can improve productivity, reduce stress, and improve overall job satisfaction by providing employees access to these tools and encouraging their use.

Encourage Regular Breaks

Taking regular breaks is essential for effective time management in the workplace. Encouraging employees to take breaks can help to reduce stress, increase productivity, and improve overall job satisfaction.

It's important to provide employees with a comfortable break area and encourage them to take short breaks throughout the day. It can help them recharge, refocus, and return to their work feeling refreshed and energized.

Avoid Multitasking

Multitasking can be a significant time-waster in the workplace. Encouraging employees to focus on one task at a time can help to improve productivity and reduce stress.

It can involve setting specific times for checking emails, avoiding distractions such as social media or unnecessary meetings, and setting boundaries around when employees are expected to be available for work-related tasks.

Provide Opportunities for Professional Development

Providing opportunities for professional development can be an effective way to improve time management in the workplace. It can involve training programs, mentoring, and coaching sessions that help employees develop skills in time management, prioritization, and productivity.

Organizations can improve productivity, reduce stress, and improve job satisfaction by providing employees with the skills and tools to manage their time effectively.

In conclusion, implementing time management strategies in the workplace is essential for improving productivity, reducing stress, and improving job satisfaction. By setting clear goals and priorities, creating a schedule, using time management tools and techniques, encouraging regular breaks, avoiding multitasking, and providing opportunities for professional development, organizations can help employees manage their time effectively and achieve success in their roles.

CHAPTER FIVE

LEADERSHIP

Leadership is crucial to success as it involves inspiring and motivating others, setting a clear direction and vision, making effective decisions, and fostering collaboration and innovation, leading to extraordinary organizational and personal achievement. Without effective leadership, individuals and organizations may struggle to achieve their goals and adapt to changing circumstances.

What Is Leadership?

Leadership can be defined as the ability to inspire, influence and guide others toward a common goal or vision. A leader can motivate people to work towards a common objective and has the necessary skills to make that objective a reality. In essence, leadership is about taking charge of a situation, setting a direction, and guiding others toward that direction.

Leadership can be seen in various contexts, from business to politics, sports to education, and personal relationships. It is an essential aspect of success in all areas of life. Whether you are a business owner, a politician, a coach, or a parent, the ability to inspire, influence, and guide others toward a common goal is critical for success.

Effective leadership requires strong communication skills, the ability to motivate and inspire others, the willingness to lead by example, the ability to make difficult decisions, and a commitment to continuous learning and improvement. With these qualities in mind, anyone can become an effective leader and positively impact the world around them.

Leaders understand that success is about achieving their goals and supporting and developing the people around them. By helping others, leaders can create a positive and supportive work environment, build trust and loyalty, and ultimately achieve greater success as a team.

Ultimately, leadership is about creating a culture of excellence and continuous improvement, empowering individuals and teams to take ownership of their work and strive towards their full potential. By developing practical leadership skills, individuals can achieve personal success and contribute to the success of their team, organization, and society.

Leadership In Business Management

In the world of business management, leadership is a critical component of success. Effective leaders in this context are responsible for setting the company's strategic direction, motivating employees, and making difficult decisions that impact the organization's future. Several fundamental principles of leadership are particularly important in the context of business management.

First and foremost, effective leaders in business management must be able to communicate effectively. It means articulating a clear vision for the company and ensuring all employees understand their role in achieving it. It also means being able to provide feedback and constructive criticism in a way that is clear, respectful, and actionable.

In addition to effective communication, effective leaders in business management must also be able to inspire and motivate their employees. It requires a deep understanding of what drives individual employees and the ability to connect those motivations to the organization's broader goals. Effective leaders must create a culture of accountability, where employees are encouraged to take ownership of their work and feel empowered to take risks and try new things.

Another important quality of effective leaders in business management is the ability to make difficult decisions. It might mean deciding to cut costs or restructure the organization in response to changing market conditions or investing in new technology or research and development to stay ahead of competitors. Influential leaders must be able to weigh the pros and cons of different options and make decisions that are in the best interests of the company as a whole.

Finally, effective leaders in business management must be able to adapt to changing circumstances and environments. In today's fast-paced and constantly evolving business landscape, leaders must be able to pivot quickly and adjust their strategies in response to changing market conditions, technological advances, or shifts in consumer preferences. It requires a willingness to embrace change and a commitment to continuous learning and improvement.

Leadership is essential for success in business management. Effective leaders must communicate effectively, inspire and motivate employees, make difficult decisions, and adapt to changing circumstances and environments. By embodying these leadership principles, business managers can build strong, resilient organizations capable of achieving long-term success in a rapidly changing world.

How to Improve Leadership Skills?

Leadership skills are not something that you are born with but rather something that you can develop over time. There are several tips and strategies that you can use to improve your leadership skills and become a more effective leader.

Develop Your Communication Skills

Effective communication is essential for effective leadership. You must clearly articulate your vision, goals, and expectations to your team members. Take the time to improve your public speaking, writing, and listening skills to communicate more effectively with your team.

Build Relationships With Your Team Members

Effective leaders build strong relationships with their team members. Take the time to get to know your team members personally and show them that you care about their success and well-being. It will help to build trust and loyalty and make your team members more willing to follow your lead.

Lead By Example

Effective leaders lead by example. You need to model the behavior and attitudes that you want your team members to adopt. Be punctual, reliable, and hardworking, and show your team members that you are willing to roll up your sleeves and get your hands dirty.

Be Open To Feedback

Effective leaders are open to feedback from their team members. Encourage your team members to share their ideas, concerns, and feedback with you, and be willing to listen and act on their feedback. It will help to build a culture of collaboration and innovation and make your team members feel valued and respected.

Learn From Your Mistakes

Effective leaders are not perfect, and they make mistakes from time to time. When you make a mistake, take the time to reflect on what went wrong and what you can do differently in the future. Use your mistakes as an opportunity to learn and grow, and show your team members that you are willing to admit your mistakes and take responsibility for them.

Invest In Your Development

Effective leaders are committed to their development. Take the time to read books, attend seminars and conferences, and take courses that will help you to improve your leadership skills. The more you invest in your development, the more you can inspire and motivate your team members.

In conclusion, improving your leadership skills is a continuous process. By developing your communication skills, building relationships with your team members, leading by example, being open to feedback, learning from your mistakes, and investing in your development, you can become a more effective leader and inspire your team members to achieve their goals.

Importance Of Leadership In The Workplace

Leadership is a critical component of success in the workplace. Influential leaders are responsible for setting the organization's strategic direction, motivating employees, and creating a positive and productive work environment. There are several key reasons why leadership is important in the workplace.

First and foremost, effective leadership is essential for achieving organizational goals. Leaders are responsible for setting the organization's vision, mission, and goals and ensuring that all employees understand their role in achieving those goals. Effective leaders can create a sense of purpose and direction for the organization and provide the guidance and support employees need to succeed.

In addition to achieving organizational goals, effective leadership is also important for creating a positive and productive work environment. Leaders who can inspire and motivate their employees to develop a culture of accountability, where employees are encouraged to take ownership of their work and feel empowered to take risks and try new things. It leads to greater job satisfaction, employee engagement, and overall productivity.

Effective leadership is also important for employee development and growth. Leaders who provide feedback and constructive criticism help employees improve their skills and develop new competencies. It creates a learning and continuous improvement culture where employees are encouraged to take on new challenges and build their careers.

Another important aspect of effective leadership is managing conflict and resolving disputes. In any workplace, there will inevitably be disagreements and conflicts that arise. Leaders who can handle these conflicts constructively and respectfully help create a positive and productive work environment where all employees feel valued and respected.

Finally, effective leadership is important for creating a culture of innovation and creativity. Leaders who foster a culture of experimentation and risk-taking help employees think outside the box and develop new and innovative ideas. It leads to greater innovation, creativity, and competitiveness in the marketplace.

In conclusion, effective leadership is essential for success in the workplace. Influential leaders are responsible for achieving organizational goals, creating a positive and productive work environment, developing and growing employees, managing conflict and disputes, and fostering a culture of innovation and creativity. By embodying these leadership principles, organizations can build strong, resilient teams capable of achieving long-term success in a rapidly changing world.

Examples Of Strong Leadership Skills

Leaders come from different backgrounds, cultures, and political systems. They hold various positions of power, such as presidents, prime ministers, monarchs, and religious leaders. Some leaders have left a lasting impact on history, while others are relatively unknown outside their respective countries.

Leaders have a tremendous responsibility to their citizens and the global community. The best leaders lead with integrity, compassion, and a strong sense of purpose, inspiring their followers to work toward a better future for all.

Mahatma Gandhi

Gandhi is considered one of the greatest leaders in history for his ability to lead India to independence from British rule through nonviolent civil disobedience. His approach to leadership emphasized selflessness, empathy, and a deep commitment to social justice.

Nelson Mandela

Mandela's leadership skills were demonstrated during his time as president of South Africa, where he successfully led the country through a peaceful transition from apartheid to democracy. His ability to unite people and inspire them to work towards a common goal is a testament to his strong leadership.

Winston Churchill

Churchill's leadership skills were demonstrated during World War II when he led Britain through some of its darkest hours. His ability to inspire and motivate people to fight for their country and freedom is a testament to his strong leadership.

Bill Gates

Bill Gates is widely recognized as one of modern history's most successful business leaders. As the co-founder of Microsoft, he played a critical role in developing the personal computer industry and revolutionizing how people use technology. His leadership style is focused, strategic, and results-oriented, emphasizing innovation and forward thinking.

Steve Jobs

Steve Jobs was a visionary leader who transformed the technology industry with innovative products and marketing strategies. His strong leadership skills demonstrate his ability to inspire and motivate his team members to create products that change the world.

Elon Musk

Musk is the CEO of SpaceX and Tesla, and his leadership skills have been instrumental in revolutionizing the space and automotive industries. His ability to inspire and motivate his team members to think big and take risks has helped to create some of the most innovative products in the world.

CHAPTER SIX

DETERMINATION

Determination can lead to success by providing the necessary motivation, resilience, discipline, self-confidence, and growth mindset to overcome obstacles and persist in achieving one's goals.

What Is Determination?

Determination is the quality of being firm in one's purpose or intent. It involves a strong desire and willingness to pursue one's goals despite obstacles, setbacks, and difficulties. Determination is crucial to success in any field, whether in academics, sports, business, or personal development.

A determined person is highly motivated, disciplined, and focused on their goals. They possess an unwavering commitment to their objectives and are willing to put in the effort and time required to achieve them. A determined individual has a clear vision of what they want to accomplish, and they work tirelessly towards that vision until it is realized.

The importance of determination cannot be overstated. Individuals will likely falter without determination when faced with obstacles, setbacks, or failures. It is the driving force behind resilience, perseverance, and grit. It provides the necessary fuel to overcome obstacles and achieve success, regardless of the challenges.

One of the key characteristics of determination is perseverance. Perseverance involves the ability to persist in the face of adversity. The quality enables an individual to keep going despite setbacks and failures. A determined person understands that failure is not the end but a stepping stone toward success. They use failure as an opportunity to learn and grow rather than a reason to give up.

Another essential characteristic of determination is self-discipline. Self-discipline involves controlling one's thoughts, emotions, and behaviors. It requires delaying gratification and focusing on long-term goals rather than short-term pleasures. A determined individual is highly self-disciplined and understands that success requires sacrifice and hard work.

Finally, determination requires a positive mindset. A positive mindset involves having a belief in oneself and one's abilities. It involves taking risks, embracing challenges, and persevering in adversity. A determined person has a positive outlook on life and sees obstacles as opportunities rather than barriers.

In conclusion, determination is a crucial quality for success in any field. It involves perseverance, self-discipline, and a positive mindset. A determined individual is highly motivated, focused, and committed to their goals. They understand that success requires hard work, sacrifice, and a willingness to overcome obstacles. With determination, anything is possible, and success is within reach.

How Can Determination Lead To Success?

Determination is the fuel that propels an individual toward success. The quality separates those who achieve their goals from those who give up at the first sign of difficulty. Determination can lead to success in several ways.

Firstly, determination provides the necessary motivation to overcome obstacles. Success is rarely easy. It requires hard work, sacrifice, and persistence. Determination motivates a person to keep going even when things get tough. It enables individuals to push through the challenges and setbacks that inevitably arise on the path to success.

Secondly, determination fosters resilience. Resilience is the ability to bounce back from setbacks and failures. It involves a willingness to learn from mistakes and to use them as opportunities for growth. Determination helps individuals to develop resilience by providing the strength and courage to keep going in the face of adversity.

Thirdly, determination encourages discipline. Discipline is essential for success in any field. It involves controlling one's thoughts, emotions, and behaviors. The determination provides the discipline required to stay focused on long-term goals, prioritize tasks, and manage time effectively.

Fourthly, determination leads to increased self-confidence. Self-confidence is the belief in oneself and one's abilities. It is a critical factor in achieving success. A determined person who has overcome obstacles and achieved their goals will naturally feel more self-confident. This increased self-confidence can lead to further success as the individual takes on new challenges positively.

Finally, determination fosters a growth mindset. A growth mindset believes hard work and dedication can develop intelligence, skills, and abilities. It involves a willingness to embrace challenges and to view failures as opportunities for growth. Determination helps individuals to develop a growth mindset by encouraging them to persist in the face of difficulties and to see setbacks as opportunities for learning and improvement.

In conclusion, a determination is a critical factor in achieving success. It provides the motivation, resilience, discipline, self-confidence, and growth mindset to overcome obstacles and achieve goals. With determination, individuals can push through the challenges and setbacks that arise on the path to success and achieve their dreams.

How To Be Determined Towards Your Goal?

Determining your goal requires a combination of mindset, habits, and actions.

Here are some practical steps you can take to increase your determination toward your goals:

Define Your Goal Clearly

Start by defining your goal in detail. It means setting specific, measurable, achievable, relevant, and time-bound (SMART) goals. Focusing your energy and effort toward that goal becomes easier when you clearly understand what you want to achieve.

Create A Plan

Once you have defined your goal, create an action plan outlining the steps you need to take to achieve your goal. Break down your goal into smaller, manageable tasks that you can work on every day.

Stay Focused

Staying focused on your goal is essential to maintain your determination. Eliminate distractions such as social media or other non-essential activities that may hinder your progress. Prioritize your time and energy on the tasks that will bring you closer to your goal.

Build Resilience

Building resilience is crucial when it comes to staying determined toward your goal. Expect setbacks, and be prepared to face them with a positive mindset. Learn from your mistakes and failures and use them as opportunities to grow.

Develop Positive Habits

Positive habits can help you stay determined toward your goal. Make a habit of working towards your goal every day, even if it's only for a short time. Practice positive self-talk, visualization, and affirmations to boost your motivation and confidence.

Stay Accountable

Staying accountable to yourself and others can help you stay determined toward your goal. Share your goal with others and ask them to hold you accountable. Set deadlines and milestones to track your progress.

Celebrate Your Successes

Celebrating your successes, no matter how small can help you stay motivated and determined toward your goal. Take time to acknowledge and reward yourself for the progress you have made.

In conclusion, being determined toward your goal requires a combination of mindset, habits, and actions. By defining your goal clearly, creating a plan, staying focused, building resilience, developing positive habits, staying accountable, and celebrating your successes, you can increase your determination and achieve your goals.

CHAPTER SEVEN

EXPERTISE AND EXCELLENCE

Expertise and excellence are essential to achieving success. Expertise provides the foundation of knowledge and skills necessary to perform a task effectively, while excellence involves a commitment to delivering consistently high-quality results.

Expertise and Excellence

Expertise and excellence are closely related concepts often used interchangeably but have distinct meanings. While both concepts are essential for success, their focus and scope differ.

Expertise refers to an individual's knowledge, skills, and experience in a particular area or field. It is the product of deliberate practice and learning over time, which results in a deep understanding of a subject matter. Expertise is acquired through education, training, mentorship, and practical experience. An expert in a field possesses a knowledge and understanding that exceeds that of a novice or an amateur.

Conversely, excellence refers to the quality of work or performance that is exceptional or superior to others. It results from a consistent and sustained effort to achieve a high level of proficiency in a particular area. Excellence is not just about achieving a high level of skill or knowledge but also about delivering consistently high-quality results over time. A person who strives for excellence is committed to doing their best, pushing themselves beyond their limits, and continually improving their performance.

While expertise and excellence are distinct concepts, they are closely related and often go hand in hand. An individual with expertise in a particular field has the knowledge and skills to achieve excellence. Conversely, someone striving for excellence will likely acquire expertise over time.

Expertise is the foundation of excellence. Without expertise, it isn't easy to achieve high-quality results consistently. Expertise provides the necessary knowledge and skills to effectively perform a task or solve a problem. It also enables individuals to anticipate and prepare for potential challenges and obstacles.

Excellence, on the other hand, is the product of deliberate practice and continuous improvement. It requires a commitment to excellence and a willingness to go above and beyond the minimum requirements. Excellence involves setting high standards, consistently delivering high-quality work, and continually seeking to improve performance.

In summary, both expertise and excellence require sustained effort, deliberate practice, and a commitment to continuous improvement. By striving for knowledge and excellence, individuals can achieve exceptional results in their chosen field and significantly contribute to society.

How To Be Excellent In Everything You Do?

Here are some key points to consider to be excellent in everything you do:

Set High Standards

Define what excellence means to you and set high standards for yourself. Establish clear expectations for the quality of work you want to produce.

Focus On The Process

Rather than focusing solely on the end result, focus on the process of achieving it. Pay attention to the details, and take the necessary steps to ensure the process is efficient and effective.

Continuously Improve

Make a habit of continuous learning and improving. Seek feedback from others, reflect on your performance, and actively seek growth opportunities.

Manage Your Time Effectively

Time management is critical in achieving excellence. Prioritize your tasks, set realistic deadlines, and eliminate any distractions hindering your progress.

Be Proactive

Take the initiative to identify and solve problems before they become bigger issues. Anticipate potential obstacles and prepare for them in advance.

Embrace Challenges

Challenges are opportunities to learn and grow. Embrace them with a positive mindset and a willingness to step outside your comfort zone.

Collaborate With Others

Collaboration can help you achieve excellence by leveraging the strengths and expertise of others. Seek out opportunities to work with others and learn from their perspectives.

Be Accountable

Take ownership of your work and be accountable for the results. Set clear goals, measure your progress, and take responsibility for any mistakes or setbacks.

Practice Self-Discipline

Self-discipline is essential for achieving excellence. Develop habits and routines that support your goals, and stay committed to them even when challenging.

Celebrate Successes

Take time to celebrate your successes, no matter how small. Acknowledge your progress, and use it as motivation to continue striving for excellence.

In summary, achieving excellence requires a combination of mindset, habits, and actions. By setting high standards, focusing on the process, continuously improving, managing your time effectively, being proactive, embracing challenges, collaborating with others, being accountable, practicing self-discipline, and celebrating successes, you can strive for excellence in everything you do.

What Is Professional Excellence In The Workplace?

Professional excellence in the workplace consistently demonstrates high-quality performance, a commitment to excellence, and a dedication to achieving personal and organizational goals. It is characterized by a strong work ethic, a positive attitude, and a willingness to go above and beyond the minimum requirements.

Professional excellence encompasses various skills and attributes, including technical expertise, communication skills, leadership qualities, and a commitment to continuous improvement. Professionals who excel in the workplace are highly respected by their peers, admired by their superiors, and valued by their clients or customers.

Here are some key components of professional excellence in the workplace:

Technical Expertise

Professionals who excel in the workplace possess a high level of technical expertise. They deeply understand their industry and the specific tasks and responsibilities required of their job. They stay up-to-date with industry trends, technologies, and best practices.

Communication Skills

Effective communication is essential for professional excellence in the workplace. Excellent professionals can communicate clearly and effectively with colleagues, clients, and stakeholders. They listen actively, ask questions, and provide constructive feedback.

Leadership Qualities

Professionals who excel in the workplace exhibit strong leadership qualities. They can inspire and motivate others to achieve their goals. They lead by example, set high standards for themselves and others, and provide guidance and support when needed.

Commitment To Continuous Improvement

Professionals who excel in the workplace are committed to continuous improvement. They seek opportunities for growth and development and actively pursue new skills and knowledge. They are open to feedback and use it to improve their performance.

Positive Attitude

A positive attitude is essential for professional excellence in the workplace. Excellent professionals approach their work with enthusiasm, optimism, and a can-do attitude. They are resilient despite setbacks and maintain a positive outlook even when things are challenging.

Customer Focus

Professionals who excel in the workplace are customer-focused. They understand their clients‘ or customers’ needs and expectations and strive to exceed them. They are responsive, proactive, and solutions-oriented.

Accountability

Professionals who excel in the workplace are accountable for their actions and decisions. They take ownership of their work and mistakes and are willing to take responsibility for the outcomes.

Achieving professional excellence in the workplace requires a combination of mindset, skills, and behaviors. It requires a commitment to ongoing learning and development, a willingness to take on challenges, and a dedication to delivering high-quality work. Professionals who excel in the workplace are valued for their technical expertise, leadership qualities, communication skills, and positive attitude.

In conclusion, professional excellence in the workplace results from hard work, dedication, and a commitment to ongoing learning and development. Technical expertise, effective communication, strong leadership qualities, a commitment to continuous improvement, a positive attitude, customer focus, and accountability characterize it. By striving for professional excellence, individuals can achieve personal and organizational success.

CHAPTER EIGHT

LISTENER

Listening is a crucial part of success as it allows individuals to understand the needs and perspectives of others, make informed decisions, and build strong relationships.

Is It Important To Be A Good Listener?

Being a good listener is crucial to effective communication and building strong relationships. Listening skills are essential in various aspects of life, including personal relationships, professional settings, and even social situations.

The following are some reasons why being a good listener is important:

Building Strong Relationships

Listening is a fundamental component of building strong and meaningful relationships. When we listen attentively to others, we show that we respect and value them. We understand their perspective and can appreciate their point of view. Being a good listener helps to foster trust, mutual respect, and understanding in relationships.

Enhancing Understanding

Listening attentively to others allows us to understand their thoughts, feelings, and ideas. We may miss important information, misinterpret messages, or make incorrect assumptions when not actively listening. By being good listeners, we can avoid misunderstandings, improve our understanding of others, and increase our overall knowledge and awareness.

Resolving Conflicts

Conflict is inevitable in any relationship, but good listening skills can help to resolve conflicts more effectively. Active listening lets us understand the other person's perspective, concerns, and needs. It helps to build empathy and creates an environment where both parties can work together to find a mutually beneficial solution.

Improving Communication

Good communication requires both speaking and listening skills. When we are good listeners, we can better communicate our thoughts and ideas effectively. Listening allows us to clarify our understanding of the message, ask relevant questions, and provide meaningful feedback.

Learning from Others

Listening to others allows us to learn from their experiences, knowledge, and wisdom. We can gain new insights, perspectives, and ideas we may not have considered before. Good listening skills also enable us to ask questions, seek clarification, and expand our understanding of a topic.

Achieving Personal Growth

Good listening skills can also help us achieve personal growth. By listening to feedback, we can identify areas for improvement, learn from our mistakes, and become more self-aware. Listening to others' stories and experiences can help us appreciate different perspectives and cultures better.

In conclusion, being a good listener is essential for success in various aspects of life. It enables us to build strong relationships, enhance our understanding of others, resolve conflicts, improve communication, learn from others, and achieve personal growth. By developing good listening skills, we can become more effective communicators, build stronger relationships, and lead more fulfilling lives.

What Makes Someone An Effective Listener?

Here are some points that make someone an effective listener:

Paying Attention

Effective listeners pay attention to the speaker, focusing on what they say.

Nonverbal Communication

Body language and nonverbal cues such as eye contact, nodding, and facial expressions show the listener is engaged and interested in the conversation.

Asking Questions

An effective listener asks relevant questions to clarify and better understand what the speaker is saying.

Avoiding Distractions

An effective listener avoids distractions such as phones, computers, or other interruptions distracting from the conversation.

Demonstrating Empathy

An effective listener shows empathy by acknowledging the speaker's feelings and emotions and responding in a way that shows he understands and cares.

Avoiding Judgment

An effective listener suspends judgment and avoids making assumptions or drawing conclusions before hearing the speaker's entire message.

Providing Feedback

An effective listener provides feedback to the speaker to ensure they are understood and confirm that the listener is engaged in the conversation.

Active Listening

An effective listener practices active listening, which involves fully concentrating on the speaker, interpreting their message accurately, and responding appropriately.

Summarizing

An effective listener summarizes the speaker's main points to ensure he understands the message correctly.

Being Present

An effective listener is present in the moment and fully engaged in the conversation, showing that he values the speaker and his message.

Why Is Being A Good Listener Important In The Workplace?

Being a good listener is important in the workplace for various reasons. Effective communication is key to building strong relationships and achieving organizational success.

Here are some reasons why being a good listener is especially important in the workplace:

Builds Trust

Employees who feel heard and understood are likelier to trust their colleagues and managers. Being a good listener helps to foster a culture of trust and respect, which can improve employee morale, engagement, and productivity.

Improves Communication

Listening is a two-way process; effective communication requires speaking and listening skills. When employees are good listeners, they can better understand their colleagues' needs and concerns and respond in a helpful and productive way.

Enhances Problem-Solving

Many workplace issues require collaboration and teamwork to solve. A good listener allows employees to gather information, understand different perspectives, and work together to solve complex problems.

Supports Professional Development

Good listening skills are essential for professional development. Employees who listen actively to feedback, advice, and guidance from colleagues and managers are better equipped to improve their skills and knowledge and ultimately advance in their careers.

Improves Customer Service

Listening is a critical component of providing excellent customer service. When employees listen actively to customer feedback, they can better understand their needs and concerns and respond helpfully and responsively.

Reduces Conflict

Workplace conflicts can be disruptive and counterproductive. A good listener allows employees to understand each other's perspectives and concerns and work together to find mutually beneficial solutions.

Demonstrates Leadership

Being a good listener is an important leadership trait. Leaders who listen to their employees demonstrate that they value their opinions and are invested in their success. It can improve employee morale and increase loyalty and commitment to the organization.

In conclusion, being a good listener is important in the workplace because it builds trust, improves communication, enhances problem-solving, supports professional development, improves customer service, reduces conflict, and demonstrates leadership. By developing strong listening skills, employees can improve their relationships with colleagues and customers, achieve tremendous career success, and contribute to a more productive and positive work environment.

CHAPTER NINE

STRONG COMMUNICATOR

Strong communication skills are essential for success in any field, enabling individuals to effectively convey their ideas, build strong relationships, and achieve their goals.

Why Is Being A Strong Communicator Important?

Being a strong communicator is important in both personal and professional life. Effective communication allows individuals to convey their thoughts, ideas, and feelings clearly and efficiently, leading to better relationships, more successful collaboration, and increased productivity.

Here are some reasons why being a strong communicator is important:

Building Relationships

Strong communication skills allow individuals to build strong and meaningful relationships with others. It can lead to better personal relationships and more successful professional relationships with colleagues, clients, and stakeholders.

Resolving Conflicts

Conflicts are a natural part of any relationship or work environment, and strong communication skills are necessary for constructively resolving these conflicts. Effective communication can help to prevent misunderstandings and miscommunications, reducing the likelihood of conflicts arising.

Increasing Productivity

Strong communication skills can help individuals to work more efficiently and effectively, reducing the likelihood of mistakes and improving overall productivity. It can lead to greater success and achievement in both personal and professional life.

Enhancing Teamwork

In many work environments, teamwork is essential for achieving success. Strong communication skills are critical for effective teamwork, allowing individuals to work together more efficiently and collaboratively.

Improving Leadership Skills

Good communication skills are essential for effective leadership. Leaders who communicate clearly and effectively can inspire and motivate their team, leading to greater success and achievement.

Building Trust

Strong communication skills are essential for building trust with others. When individuals can communicate clearly and honestly, they are more likely to be trusted by their colleagues, clients, and stakeholders.

Enhancing Personal Development

Good communication skills are essential for personal development, allowing individuals to express their thoughts and ideas more clearly and effectively. It can lead to greater self-confidence and personal growth.

In conclusion, being a strong communicator is essential for success in both personal and professional life. Effective communication allows individuals to build relationships, resolve conflicts, increase productivity, enhance teamwork, improve leadership skills, build trust, and enhance personal development. By developing strong communication skills, individuals can achieve greater success and fulfillment in all aspects of their lives.

What Are Strong Communication Skills?

Strong communication skills are a set of abilities that enable individuals to convey information, thoughts, feelings, and ideas clearly and effectively. Effective communication is essential in both personal and professional life, and strong communication skills can help individuals to build relationships, resolve conflicts, enhance teamwork, increase productivity, and achieve success.

Here are some of the key components of strong communication skills:

Clarity

One of the most important aspects of strong communication skills is clarity. Clear communication means the message is delivered concisely, straightforwardly, and easily understood. It also means avoiding ambiguous language or complex terms that may confuse the listener.

Active Listening

Strong communicators are also skilled listeners. Active listening involves paying attention to the speaker, asking clarifying questions, and summarizing what was said to ensure understanding. It helps to prevent misunderstandings and improves communication overall.

Empathy

Empathy is understanding and relating to another person's feelings or situation. Strong communicators can show empathy by acknowledging the other person's feelings and responding thoughtfully and compassionately.

Confidence

Confidence is important for effective communication. Strong communicators can speak clearly and confidently, even in challenging situations. It helps to convey a sense of authority and credibility and inspires confidence in the listener.

Non-Verbal Communication

Non-verbal communication includes facial expressions, body language, and tone of voice. Strong communicators can use non-verbal cues to convey their message effectively and to read the non-verbal cues of others to understand their message better.

Adaptability

Strong communicators are adaptable and can adjust their communication style to meet the listener's needs. It includes tailoring the message to the listener's level of knowledge, using appropriate language, and adapting the tone of voice to match the situation.

Assertiveness

Assertiveness is the ability to express oneself clearly, directly, and respectfully. Strong communicators can be assertive without being aggressive and communicate their needs, desires, and opinions in a way that is respectful and considerate of others.

Emotional Intelligence

Emotional intelligence refers to the ability to identify, understand, and manage one's own emotions and the emotions of others. Strong communicators can use emotional intelligence to navigate difficult conversations, build rapport with others, and establish trust.

In conclusion, strong communication skills are essential for success in both personal and professional life. Effective communication requires clarity, active listening, empathy, confidence, non-verbal communication, adaptability, assertiveness, and emotional intelligence. By developing these skills, individuals can become better communicators, build stronger relationships, and achieve greater success in all areas of their lives.

How To Become An Effective Communicator?

Effective communication is an essential skill in both personal and professional life.

Here are some tips to help you become a more effective communicator:

Practice Active Listening

Effective communication begins with active listening. It means paying attention to the speaker, asking clarifying questions, and summarizing what was said to ensure understanding. Practice active listening in personal and professional situations to improve your communication skills.

Tailor Your Message To Your Audience

Effective communicators tailor their message to their audience. It means using language and terminology appropriate for the listener's level of knowledge, adapting your tone of voice to match the situation, and using examples that the listener can relate to.

Use Clear And Concise Language

Effective communication requires clear and concise language. Avoid using jargon or complex terms that may confuse the listener. Use simple language that is easy to understand.

Pay Attention To Non-Verbal Communication

Non-verbal communication includes facial expressions, body language, and tone of voice. Pay attention to your non-verbal cues to ensure that they are conveying the right message, and pay attention to the non-verbal cues of others to better understand their message.

Be Confident

Confidence is important for effective communication. Speak clearly and confidently, even in challenging situations. It helps to convey a sense of authority and credibility and inspires confidence in the listener.

Practice Empathy

Empathy is understanding and relating to another person's feelings or situation. Practice empathy by acknowledging the other person's feelings and responding in a thoughtful and compassionate manner.

Be Assertive

Assertiveness is the ability to express oneself clearly, directly, and respectfully. Be assertive without being aggressive, and communicate your needs, desires, and opinions in a way that is respectful and considerate of others.

Seek Feedback

Seek feedback from others to improve your communication skills. Ask for feedback from colleagues, friends, and family, and be open to constructive criticism.

Use Technology Wisely

Technology has changed the way we communicate, but it's important to use it wisely. Use email, instant messaging, and social media when appropriate, but be aware of these communication limitations.

Practice, Practice, Practice

Like any skill, effective communication requires practice. Look for opportunities to practice your communication skills in personal and professional situations. Attend public speaking events, take communication classes, and practice communicating with different types of people.

In conclusion, becoming an effective communicator requires practice, patience, and a willingness to learn.

CHAPTER TEN

RESILIENCE

Resilience is essential for success, as it allows individuals to bounce back from setbacks, adapt to changing circumstances, and persist in facing challenges.

What Is Resilience?

Resilience is the ability to bounce back from challenging situations. It is the capacity to cope with stress, adversity, and uncertainty positively and effectively. Resilience allows individuals to adapt to changing circumstances, recover from setbacks, and maintain a sense of hope and optimism even in difficult circumstances.

Resilience is not a fixed trait that some people have, and others do not. Instead, it is a set of skills and abilities that can be developed and strengthened over time. Some factors contributing to resilience include a supportive social network, a positive outlook, effective coping strategies, and the ability to identify and utilize available resources.

Resilience is important for both personal and professional success. In personal life, resilience helps individuals to cope with stress, maintain positive relationships, and achieve personal goals. In the workplace, resilience helps employees to manage stress and conflict, adapt to change, and maintain productivity and engagement.

Some key characteristics of resilient individuals include:

Optimism

Resilient individuals tend to have a positive outlook and believe in their ability to overcome challenges.

Flexibility

Resilient individuals can adapt to changing circumstances and are willing to try new things.

Social Support

Resilient individuals have a strong social network and can seek support and help from others when needed.

Problem-Solving Skills

Resilient individuals can identify and address problems in a proactive and effective way.

Self-Care

Resilient individuals prioritize self-care activities such as exercise, healthy eating, and adequate sleep.

To develop resilience, individuals can take some steps:

Practice Self-Reflection

Take time to reflect on past experiences and identify strengths and weaknesses.

Build A Support Network

Develop positive relationships with friends, family, and colleagues.

Develop Effective Coping Strategies

Identify and utilize healthy coping strategies such as exercise, meditation, or talking to a therapist.

Maintain A Positive Outlook

Focus on the positive aspects of situations and develop a sense of hope and optimism.

Practice Mindfulness

Mindfulness practices such as meditation or deep breathing can help individuals to stay focused, calm, and centered.

In conclusion, resilience is a key factor in personal and professional success. It is the ability to adapt to changing circumstances, bounce back from setbacks, and maintain a sense of hope and optimism even in the face of adversity. Individuals can strengthen their resilience and achieve greater success in all areas of life by developing key characteristics such as optimism, flexibility, social support, problem-solving skills, and self-care.

Why Is Resilience Important For Success?

Resilience is a crucial trait that plays an important role in achieving success. The ability to recover from setbacks, adapt to changing circumstances, and persist in adversity is essential for achieving personal and professional goals.

Here are some reasons why resilience is important for success:

Helps Individuals To Overcome Obstacles

Obstacles and setbacks are a part of life, and resilient individuals are better equipped to deal with these challenges. Resilient individuals can bounce back from setbacks, stay focused on their goals, and find ways to overcome obstacles.

Improves Mental Health

Resilience is closely linked to mental health; resilient individuals are better equipped to deal with stress and anxiety. Resilience helps individuals manage stress healthily, improving overall well-being and reducing the risk of mental health problems such as depression and anxiety.

Improves Performance

Resilience is an important factor in achieving success in the workplace. Resilient individuals can adapt to changing circumstances, stay focused on their goals, and maintain productivity despite challenges. It can lead to better job performance, increased job satisfaction, and greater success in achieving career goals.

Promotes A Positive Attitude

Resilient individuals tend to have a positive outlook on life, which can improve overall well-being and lead to greater success. A positive attitude can help individuals to stay focused on their goals, find solutions to problems, and maintain a sense of hope and optimism even in the face of adversity.

Improves Relationships

Resilient individuals are better equipped to deal with conflict and maintain positive relationships. Resilience helps individuals to communicate effectively, stay focused on solutions rather than problems, and maintain a positive attitude even in difficult situations. It can lead to stronger relationships, better communication, and greater success in personal and professional life.

In conclusion, resilience is essential for success in all areas of life. The ability to recover from setbacks, adapt to changing circumstances, and maintain a positive attitude is crucial for achieving personal and professional goals. By developing resilience through effective coping strategies, building a support network, and maintaining a positive outlook, individuals can overcome obstacles and achieve greater success in all areas of life.

Why Is Resilience Important In Leadership?

Resilience is an important trait for leaders, as it helps them navigate the challenges and uncertainties of leading a team or organization.

Here are some reasons why resilience is important in leadership:

Helps Leaders To Stay Focused On Their Goals

Resilient leaders are better equipped to stay focused on their goals, despite setbacks and challenges. Resilient leaders can maintain a clear vision of what they want to achieve and are better equipped to make decisions to help them achieve their goals.

Helps Leaders To Inspire Others

Resilient leaders can inspire others to persevere in the face of adversity. By demonstrating their resilience, leaders can help create a culture of resilience within their team or organization, leading to greater success.

Helps Leaders To Adapt To Change

Leaders must quickly adapt to changing circumstances in today's fast-paced business environment. Resilient leaders are better equipped to handle unexpected changes and adapt to new situations, which can help their team or organization to stay competitive and succeed.

Helps Leaders To Manage Stress

Leadership can be stressful and demanding, and resilient leaders are better equipped to manage stress healthily. By maintaining a positive outlook and developing effective coping strategies, resilient leaders can avoid burnout and maintain their effectiveness over the long term.

Helps Leaders To Make Better Decisions

Resilient leaders can make better decisions, even amid uncertainty and ambiguity. By maintaining a clear and focused mindset, resilient leaders can better evaluate options and make decisions in their team's or organization's best interests.

In conclusion, resilience is essential for leaders, as it helps them navigate the challenges and uncertainties of leading a team or organization. By staying focused on their goals, inspiring others, adapting to change, managing stress, and making better decisions, resilient leaders can create a culture of resilience within their team or organization, leading to greater success.

CHAPTER ELEVEN

WILLINGNESS TO LEARN

A willingness to learn is essential for success. It allows individuals to continuously develop their skills and knowledge, adapt to new situations, and remain relevant in a constantly changing world. Embracing a growth mindset and seeking new learning opportunities can lead to significant personal and professional achievements.

What Is A Commitment To Learning?

A commitment to learning is a mindset or approach individuals adopt when they are dedicated to continuously improving their knowledge, skills, and abilities. Investing in oneself is a deliberate and conscious decision, recognizing that learning is a lifelong journey and not just a means to an end.

At its core, a commitment to learning involves a willingness to take on new challenges, embrace feedback and constructive criticism, and seek opportunities for growth and development. It is a proactive approach to personal and professional development, where individuals take ownership of their learning and actively seek resources, mentors, and experiences to help them achieve their goals.

There are several key components of a commitment to learning. One of the most important is a growth mindset, which is the belief that skills and abilities can be developed through effort and perseverance. Individuals with a growth mindset view challenges as opportunities for growth and are not deterred by setbacks or failures. Instead, they use these experiences as learning opportunities, recognizing that they can use the knowledge and skills gained to improve and grow.

Another key component of a commitment to learning is self-awareness. Individuals committed to learning take the time to reflect on their strengths and weaknesses, as well as their learning styles and preferences. They use this self-knowledge to identify areas where they need to improve and seek resources and support to help them achieve their goals.

In addition to self-awareness, a commitment to learning also involves seeking feedback and constructive criticism. Individuals committed to learning are not afraid to ask for feedback from others and are open to suggestions for improvement. They use this feedback to identify areas where they can improve and adjust their approach accordingly.

Finally, a commitment to learning involves a willingness to take risks and try new things. Individuals committed to learning are not content to stay in their comfort zone but are willing to step outside to try new things and take on new challenges. They recognize that taking risks and trying new things is essential for growth and development and are willing to embrace the uncertainty and discomfort that comes with it.

In today's fast-paced and ever-changing world, a commitment to learning is more important than ever. Rapid technological advances and changes in the job market mean that individuals must constantly learn and adapt to remain competitive. A commitment to learning can help individuals stay relevant and adaptable and provide a sense of purpose and fulfillment in their personal and professional lives.

In conclusion, a commitment to learning is vital to personal and professional success. It involves a growth mindset, self-awareness, seeking feedback, and a willingness to take risks and try new things. Individuals committed to learning are better equipped to navigate the challenges of the modern world, remain relevant and adaptable, and achieve their personal and professional goals.

Why Willingness To Learn Is The Key To Success?

Willingness to learn is the key to success because it enables individuals to develop their skills and knowledge constantly, adapt to changing circumstances, and achieve their goals. In today's rapidly changing world, where technology and the job market constantly evolve, a willingness to learn is more important than ever.

Firstly, a willingness to learn enables individuals to develop their skills and knowledge, which can lead to increased job performance and career advancement. When individuals actively seek new learning opportunities, they can better understand their industry and job responsibilities, allowing them to perform better and take on new challenges. Additionally, by investing in their education and training, individuals can make themselves more attractive to employers and increase their chances of career advancement and higher salaries.

Secondly, a willingness to learn is essential for adapting to changing circumstances. In today's rapidly changing world, individuals unwilling to learn and adapt risk falling behind and becoming obsolete. By continuously learning and acquiring new skills, individuals can stay updated with industry and job market changes, making them better equipped to adapt and thrive.

Thirdly, a willingness to learn can lead to personal growth and development. When individuals actively seek new learning opportunities, they can develop new skills, expand their knowledge, and gain a deeper understanding of themselves and the world around them. It can increase confidence, resilience, and a greater sense of purpose and fulfillment in life.

Finally, a willingness to learn is essential for achieving personal and professional goals. When individuals set ambitious goals, they must be willing to learn and acquire the skills and knowledge necessary to achieve them. Without a willingness to learn and grow, individuals may become stuck in their current situation and struggle to achieve their goals.

In conclusion, a willingness to learn is the key to success. It enables individuals to develop their skills and knowledge continuously, adapt to changing circumstances, achieve their goals, and experience personal growth and development. In today's rapidly changing world, where the pace of change accelerates, a willingness to learn is more important than ever. By embracing a growth mindset and seeking new learning opportunities, individuals can position themselves for success in their personal and professional lives.

How To Demonstrate Your Willingness To Learn At Work?

Demonstrating a willingness to learn at work is essential for personal and professional growth and career advancement. By showing a commitment to learning, individuals can increase their value to their employer and position themselves for future opportunities.

Here are some ways to demonstrate your willingness to learn at work:

Ask Questions

Asking questions is a great way to demonstrate your willingness to learn. When you ask questions, you show your colleagues and superiors that you are interested in learning and improving. You can ask questions about processes, procedures, or new initiatives and seek feedback on your work.

Attend Training And Development Opportunities

Attending training and development opportunities is a great way to demonstrate your commitment to learning. Many employers offer training programs, seminars, or workshops to help you develop new skills and knowledge. Attending these opportunities shows your employer that you are invested in your personal and professional growth.

Seek Feedback

Seeking feedback from your colleagues and superiors is another way to demonstrate your willingness to learn. When you ask for feedback, you show that you are open to constructive criticism and interested in improving your performance. Use the feedback to identify areas where you can improve and adjust your approach accordingly.

Take On New Challenges

Taking on new challenges is a great way to demonstrate your willingness to learn. When you volunteer for new projects or initiatives, you show your employer that you are not afraid to step outside your comfort zone and try new things. Additionally, taking on new challenges can help you develop new skills and knowledge.

Offer To Help Others

Offering to help others is another way to demonstrate your willingness to learn. When you help your colleagues with their work, you show that you are a team player interested in learning from others. Additionally, helping others can help you develop new skills and knowledge and build relationships with your colleagues.

Take Initiative

Taking the initiative is a great way to demonstrate your willingness to learn. When you take the initiative to solve problems or improve processes, you show your employer that you are proactive and interested in making a positive impact. Additionally, taking the initiative can help you develop new skills and knowledge.

In conclusion, demonstrating a willingness to learn at work is essential for personal and professional growth and career advancement. By asking questions, attending training and development opportunities, seeking feedback, taking on new challenges, offering to help others, and taking the initiative, individuals can position themselves for career success.

CHAPTER TWELVE

DISCIPLINE

Discipline can lead to success by helping individuals develop a strong work ethic, focus on their goals, and maintain consistency in their actions and behaviors.

Is Discipline Necessary For Success?

Discipline is a crucial ingredient for success. Without discipline, achieving one's goals and aspirations is difficult and even harder to sustain over the long term. In this sense, discipline is not just a desirable but essential trait.

One reason discipline is necessary for success is that it helps individuals develop a strong work ethic. When disciplined, individuals can prioritize their tasks and manage their time effectively, allowing them to stay focused and productive. This work ethic is essential for success in any field, as it enables individuals to put in the effort and dedication required to achieve their goals.

Discipline is also necessary for success because it helps individuals focus on their goals. By setting clear goals and sticking to them, individuals can channel their energy and resources in a specific direction, which increases their chances of success. When individuals lack discipline, they may be distracted by other pursuits or tempted to give up on their goals when the going gets tough.

Another reason discipline is necessary for success is that it enables individuals to maintain consistency in their actions and behaviors. Consistency is essential for success because it builds momentum and reinforces positive habits. Individuals can stick to their plans and progress despite obstacles or setbacks when disciplined.

Finally, discipline is necessary for success because it builds character. When disciplined, individuals develop a sense of self-control and resilience, essential for success in any area of life. These qualities enable individuals to overcome adversity, persevere in the face of challenges, and stay committed to their goals even when the going gets tough.

In conclusion, discipline is a necessary ingredient for success. It helps individuals develop a strong work ethic, focus on their goals, maintain consistency in their actions and behaviors, and build character. By cultivating discipline, individuals can position themselves for success in any area of life, whether it is their career, relationships, or personal goals.

How To Discipline Yourself For Success?

Discipline is essential for success but can be challenging to develop and maintain. However, there are several strategies that individuals can use to discipline themselves for success.

Here are some ways to cultivate self-discipline:

Set Clear Goals

Setting clear goals is essential for cultivating self-discipline. Individuals with a clear vision of their goals are more likely to stay focused and motivated. Make sure your goals are specific, measurable, achievable, relevant, and time-bound. Write them down and review them regularly to keep on track.

Create A Routine

Creating a routine is another way to cultivate self-discipline. Individuals with a set routine tend to stay on task and avoid distractions. Establish a daily routine that includes time for work, exercise, self-care, and leisure activities. Stick to this routine as much as possible, even on weekends.

Prioritize Your Tasks

Prioritizing your tasks is essential for cultivating self-discipline. When individuals prioritize their tasks, they can focus on the most important and urgent tasks first, increasing their productivity and efficiency. Use a to-do list to prioritize your tasks and tackle them in order of importance.

Break Tasks Into Smaller Steps

Breaking tasks into smaller steps is another way to cultivate self-discipline. When individuals break tasks into smaller steps, they can focus on one task at a time and avoid feeling overwhelmed. Use a project management tool or a planner to break larger tasks into smaller steps and track your progress.

Practice Self-Control

Practicing self-control is essential for cultivating self-discipline. When individuals practice self-control, they can resist temptations and make choices that align with their goals. Practice self-control by avoiding distractions, saying no to unnecessary commitments, and setting boundaries with others.

Hold Yourself Accountable

Holding yourself accountable is another way to cultivate self-discipline. When individuals hold themselves accountable, they take responsibility for their actions and outcomes, which increases their motivation and commitment. Use a journal or a goal tracker to monitor your progress and hold yourself accountable for achieving your goals.

Practice Self-Care

Practicing self-care is essential for cultivating self-discipline. When you care for your physical and mental health, you are better equipped to handle challenges and focus on your goals. You must practice self-care by getting enough sleep, eating a healthy diet, exercising regularly, and taking breaks when needed.

In conclusion, discipline is essential for success but can be challenging to develop and maintain. By setting clear goals, creating a routine, prioritizing tasks, breaking tasks into smaller steps, practicing self-control, holding yourself accountable, and practicing self-care, you can discipline yourself for success. Cultivating self-discipline requires practice and commitment, but the rewards are worth the effort.

What Is The Importance Of Discipline In a Professional Career?

Discipline is an important trait to have in any professional career. It enables individuals to develop a strong work ethic, maintain focus, and achieve their goals.

Here are some ways that discipline is essential to a successful professional career:

Consistency

Discipline helps individuals maintain consistency in their actions and behaviors. It is important in a professional career because consistency builds trust and reliability. When individuals are consistent in their work, they can build a reputation for dependability, leading to promotions, raises, and new opportunities.

Time Management

Discipline also helps individuals manage their time effectively. Time management is essential in a professional career because it enables individuals to meet deadlines, stay on top of their workload, and prioritize their tasks. When individuals are disciplined with their time, they can balance competing demands and remain focused on their goals.

Goal Setting

Discipline helps individuals set clear goals and work towards them. Goal setting is essential in a professional career because it enables individuals to focus their energy and resources on achieving specific outcomes. When individuals are disciplined with goal setting, they can measure their progress, adjust their strategies, and stay motivated.

Professionalism

Discipline also contributes to professionalism in the workplace. When disciplined, individuals can maintain high professionalism when interacting with colleagues, clients, and stakeholders. It includes being punctual, courteous, and respectful and adhering to professional standards of conduct.

Adaptability

Discipline helps individuals develop adaptability in the face of change and uncertainty. In a professional career, individuals may encounter unexpected challenges, shifting priorities, and new opportunities. When disciplined, individuals can adapt to these changes and maintain a positive attitude, which can help them succeed in new and unfamiliar situations.

Self-Motivation

Discipline also helps individuals cultivate self-motivation. In a professional career, individuals may not always receive external motivation or recognition for their work. When disciplined, individuals can stay motivated and committed to their goals, even without external incentives.

In conclusion, discipline is a necessary trait to have in any professional career. It enables individuals to maintain consistency, manage their time effectively, set clear goals, maintain professionalism, adapt to change, and cultivate self-motivation. By developing discipline in their professional lives, individuals can position themselves for success and achieve their career goals.

How To Practise Self-Discipline In The Workplace?

Practicing self-discipline in the workplace is crucial to achieving success in your professional life.

Here are some ways to practice self-discipline in the workplace:

Set Clear Goals

Setting clear and specific goals can help you stay focused and motivated. When you clearly understand what you want to achieve, you can create a plan to achieve it and remain disciplined in your efforts.

Prioritize Your Tasks

Make a list of your tasks and prioritize them based on their importance and urgency. Focus on completing the most important tasks first and avoid getting distracted by less important tasks.

Avoid Procrastination

Procrastination is a major obstacle to self-discipline. Try to avoid delaying tasks and instead tackle them as soon as possible. It can help you stay on top of your workload and avoid unnecessary stress.

Limit Distractions

Distractions can disrupt your focus and make it challenging to stay disciplined. To limit distractions, turn off your phone notifications, avoid checking your emails constantly, and block access to social media during work hours.

Take Breaks

Taking regular breaks can help you recharge your energy and avoid burnout. Use your breaks to do something that helps you relax and refocus, such as taking a walk, meditating, or listening to music.

Hold Yourself Accountable

Hold yourself accountable for your actions and take responsibility for your mistakes. It can help you develop a strong sense of self-discipline and integrity.

Maintain A Positive Attitude

Maintaining a positive attitude can help you stay motivated and focused. Focus on your work's positive aspects and avoid dwelling on negative thoughts or emotions.

Seek Support

Seek support from your colleagues or supervisor if you need help staying disciplined. It can help you stay motivated and focused on your goals.

In conclusion, self-discipline is essential for success in the workplace. By setting clear goals, prioritizing tasks, avoiding procrastination, limiting distractions, taking breaks, holding yourself accountable, maintaining a positive attitude, and seeking support when necessary, you can practice self-discipline and achieve your professional goals.

CHAPTER THIRTEEN

BIG DREAMS

Dreaming big is important because it provides motivation, inspiration, and a sense of purpose. When you have a big dream, it can push you to work harder, take risks, and overcome obstacles to achieve something truly significant.

Should You Dream Big Or Be Realistic?

Whether to dream big or be realistic has been debated for many years. Some people argue that it is better to set realistic goals and work towards achieving them, while others believe that it is important to dream big and pursue lofty aspirations. Ultimately, the answer to this question will depend on the individual and their circumstances.

On the one hand, setting realistic goals can be a practical approach to achieving success. By setting achievable objectives, individuals can create a roadmap for success within their reach. It can be beneficial when dealing with short-term goals, such as completing a project or meeting a deadline. Setting realistic goals makes us more likely to succeed, which can help build confidence and momentum as we move forward.

On the other hand, dreaming big can be a powerful motivator to inspire us to achieve things we might not have thought possible. When we set our sights on a big goal, we are forced to think outside the box and devise creative solutions. It can help build resilience, persistence, and determination, all essential for success. Additionally, dreaming big can help to create a sense of purpose and passion that can drive us to work harder and overcome obstacles.

Ultimately, whether to dream big or be realistic will depend on the individual and their circumstances. Setting realistic goals and working towards achievable objectives may be the best approach for some people. For others, dreaming big and pursuing lofty aspirations may be more appropriate.

The key is to find the right balance between the two approaches and to stay focused and motivated on the path to success. Whatever approach you choose, remember that success is not a destination but a journey, and the effort and perseverance we put into that journey will ultimately define our success.

Why Is It Important To Dream Big?

Dreaming big is an important part of personal growth and development, allowing individuals to expand their horizons and explore new possibilities. When we dream big, we challenge ourselves to think beyond our current limitations and imagine a bigger and brighter future than we may have previously considered possible. It can be an incredibly empowering experience that can help to foster self-confidence, resilience, and a sense of purpose.

One of the key benefits of dreaming big is that it can help to overcome self-doubt and limiting beliefs. Many people struggle with self-doubt and negative self-talk, which can hold them back from achieving their full potential. By dreaming big, individuals can challenge these negative thought patterns and envision a more optimistic future. It can help build confidence and self-belief, which can be incredibly empowering when pursuing personal goals and ambitions.

Dreaming big can also help individuals develop a growth mindset, an important quality for personal and professional success. A growth mindset is a belief that one's abilities and intelligence can be developed through hard work, dedication, and perseverance. When individuals dream big, they are forced to embrace this growth mindset and push themselves outside their comfort zones to achieve their goals. It can help build resilience and persistence, which are essential for success in any field.

Finally, dreaming big can help individuals identify and pursue their passions and purpose. When we dream big, we are forced to consider what we truly want out of life and what we are willing to work hard to achieve. It can be an incredibly clarifying experience that can help individuals to identify their values, passions, and goals. By pursuing these things, individuals can lead more fulfilling and satisfying lives, ultimately leading to greater happiness and success.

In conclusion, dreaming big is important for personal growth and development. By challenging ourselves to think beyond our current limitations, we can build self-confidence, resilience, and a sense of purpose to help us achieve our full potential. Whether in our personal or professional lives, dreaming big can help us identify our passions, pursue our goals, and ultimately make ourselves bigger and more successful.

How To Dream Big And Achieve It?

Dreaming big is an important part of personal growth and development, but it is only the first step in achieving success. To turn our dreams into reality, we must take concrete steps to make them a reality.

Here are some tips for how to dream big and achieve it:

Set Specific Goals

It is important to break big dreams down into specific goals to achieve them. These goals should be specific, measurable, achievable, relevant, and time-bound (SMART). Setting specific goals can create a roadmap for success within our reach.

Develop A Plan

Once we have set specific goals, we must develop a plan for achieving them. This plan should include specific actions we need to take to achieve our goals and a timeline for when we expect to accomplish each step.

Stay Focused

Achieving big dreams requires focus and dedication. It is important to stay focused on our goals and not let distractions or setbacks derail us from our path. It may require sacrifices, such as giving up certain activities or habits not aligned with our goals.

Take Action

Dreams don't become a reality by themselves. We need to take action to achieve them. It may involve taking risks, trying new things, and stepping outside our comfort zones. We must be willing to take action and put in the hard work required to achieve our goals.

Stay Motivated

Achieving big dreams can be a long and challenging journey. Staying motivated and maintaining a positive attitude are important, even when faced with setbacks and obstacles. It may involve finding sources of inspiration and support, such as a mentor, a supportive network of friends and family, or motivational quotes and literature.

Learn From Failures

Failure is a natural part of the journey toward achieving big dreams. Learning from our failures and using them as opportunities to grow and improve is important. We can continue moving toward our goals by reflecting on our mistakes and adjusting to our plans.

In conclusion, achieving big dreams requires vision, planning, action, focus, motivation, and resilience. These tips can turn our dreams into reality and help us achieve our full potential.

How To Stay Motivated To Turn Your Dreams Into Reality?

Turning our dreams into reality can be a long and challenging journey. It is common to experience periods of self-doubt, frustration, and lack of motivation. However, staying motivated is essential for success.

Here are some tips for how to stay motivated to turn your dreams into reality:

Keep Your Vision In Mind

When the going gets tough, losing sight of our goals and getting bogged down in the day-to-day details can be easy. It is important to keep our vision in mind and remind ourselves of why we are pursuing our dreams in the first place. It can help provide clarity and focus and renew our motivation and purpose.

Celebrate Small Victories

Achieving big dreams requires taking many small steps along the way. Celebrating each small victory is important, as this can help build momentum and motivate us. It may involve setting mini-goals and rewarding ourselves when we achieve them or simply reflecting on our progress and feeling proud of what we have accomplished.

Surround Yourself With Positivity

Our environment can have a significant impact on our motivation levels. It is important to surround ourselves with positivity and support. It may involve seeking mentors, joining a supportive community or network, or simply spending time with friends and family who believe in us and encourage us to pursue our dreams.

Practice Self-Care

Achieving big dreams can be a long and exhausting journey. Practicing self-care and caring for our physical and emotional needs is important. It may involve getting enough sleep, eating well, exercising, and taking necessary breaks. Caring for ourselves makes us better equipped to stay motivated and focused on our goals.

Embrace Failure

Failure is a natural part of the journey toward achieving big dreams. It is important to embrace failure as a learning opportunity rather than a sign of defeat. By reframing failure as an opportunity to grow and improve, we can stay motivated and continue moving toward our goals.

In conclusion, staying motivated to turn our dreams into reality requires a combination of mindset, self-care, and support. We can stay motivated and achieve our full potential by remembering our vision, celebrating small victories, positively surrounding ourselves, practicing self-care, and embracing failure.

How Does Having A Big Dream Help You Grow As A Person?

Having a big dream can help you grow in many ways. Firstly, you must step outside your comfort zone and challenge yourself to pursue something difficult or daunting. It can help you build resilience, self-confidence, and a sense of inner strength that can serve you well in other areas.

Secondly, having a big dream requires you to develop a growth mindset where you are willing to take risks, learn from failures, and continuously improve. It can help you develop a more positive and proactive outlook on life and help you approach challenges with greater creativity, flexibility, and adaptability.

Thirdly, having a big dream can help you develop a sense of purpose and direction and give you more significant meaning and fulfillment in your life. Pursuing a big dream can help you align your actions and values and give you a sense of clarity and focus that can help you navigate the ups and downs of life with greater ease and grace.

Overall, having a big dream can help you grow in many ways and provide a sense of purpose, fulfillment, and joy that can enrich your life in countless ways.

CHAPTER FOURTEEN

EXCELLENT NETWORK

Networking is important for success because it allows individuals to connect with others in their industry or field, build relationships, gain insights and knowledge, and access opportunities that may not have been available to them otherwise.

What Are Strong Networking Skills?

Strong networking skills are essential for building meaningful connections and relationships with others, whether in a personal or professional setting.

Here are some key skills that can help individuals become effective networkers:

Active listening

Good networking requires active listening skills, which means being fully present and attentive to the person you speak with. It involves listening to their needs, interests, and goals and showing genuine interest in their perspective.

Communication

Effective networking also requires strong communication skills, including the ability to articulate your goals, interests, and needs clearly and confidently. It may involve developing an elevator pitch or concise summary of your skills and expertise and asking thoughtful questions to show interest in the other person.

Relationship-building

Networking is about building relationships, so being personable, friendly, and approachable is important. It may involve making eye contact, smiling, and finding common ground to establish a connection with the other person.

Follow-up

Building strong relationships requires follow-up and follow-through. It means taking the initiative to follow up with the people you meet through a thank-you note, email, or phone call. It also means keeping your promises and following through on your commitments.

Empathy

Finally, strong networking skills require empathy, which means being able to understand and relate to the needs and concerns of others. It may involve putting yourself in the other person's shoes, being mindful of their perspective, and showing kindness and compassion in your interactions.

Overall, strong networking skills are essential for building meaningful connections and relationships with others. By developing active listening, communication, relationship-building, follow-up, and empathy skills, individuals can become more effective networkers and build strong, long-lasting relationships to help them achieve their personal and professional goals.

Why Is Networking Important For Success?

Networking is important for success because it allows individuals to build connections and relationships, leading to new opportunities, insights, and knowledge.

Here are some key reasons why networking is important for success:

Access To Opportunities

Networking can provide individuals access to new opportunities, whether job openings, business partnerships, or collaborations. By connecting with others in their field or industry, individuals can stay informed about new developments, trends, and opportunities that may not have been available to them otherwise.

Increased Visibility And Credibility

Networking can also help individuals increase their visibility and credibility in their field or industry. By building relationships with others, individuals can establish themselves as experts or leaders, leading to new opportunities and increased recognition.

Knowledge Sharing

Networking can also facilitate knowledge sharing and learning. By connecting with others, individuals can gain insights, perspectives, and advice from others in their field or industry, which can help them expand their knowledge and skills.

Professional Development

Networking can also provide opportunities for professional development, such as attending conferences, workshops, and training sessions. By connecting with others in their field or industry, individuals can learn about new developments and best practices and gain new skills and knowledge to help them advance in their careers.

Support And Guidance

Finally, networking can provide individuals with support and guidance, particularly during challenging times or transitions. By building relationships with others, individuals can find mentors, advisors, and advocates who can offer advice, guidance, and support as they navigate their career paths.

Overall, networking is important for success because it allows individuals to build relationships, gain access to opportunities and knowledge, and develop professionally. By investing in networking, individuals can increase their visibility, credibility, and impact and build strong, long-lasting relationships to help them achieve their goals and aspirations.

How Do Leaders Develop And Use Their Network?

Leaders develop and use their network by building and maintaining relationships with others in their field or industry.

Here are some key strategies that leaders can use to develop and use their network effectively:

Attend Events

Leaders can attend industry events, conferences, and networking events to meet new people and connect with others in their field. These events provide an opportunity to learn about new developments and trends and to meet potential collaborators, mentors, or advisors.

Join Professional Organizations

Leaders can also join professional organizations in their field or industry to connect with others who share their interests and goals. These organizations often provide access to industry resources, training, and events and can help leaders build relationships and gain visibility in their field.

Build A Social Media Presence

Leaders can also use social media platforms to build networks and connect with others in their field. By sharing their insights, opinions, and perspectives online, leaders can attract followers and build relationships with others who share their interests and goals.

Mentor And Support Others

Leaders can also develop their network by mentoring and supporting others in their field or industry. By offering advice, guidance, and support to others, leaders can build strong, long-lasting relationships that can help them achieve their own goals and aspirations.

Collaborate And Partner

Finally, leaders can develop their network by collaborating and partnering with others on projects, initiatives, or business ventures. Leaders can leverage each other's strengths and expertise by working together and building relationships based on mutual trust and respect.

Overall, leaders can develop and use their network by being proactive, building and maintaining relationships with others in their field or industry, and collaborating and partnering with others to achieve shared goals. By investing in their network, leaders can access new opportunities, insights, and knowledge and build strong, long-lasting relationships to help them succeed in their careers and beyond.

How Do You Build A Strong Network At The Workplace?

Building a strong network at the workplace is essential for career growth and success.

Here are some key strategies for building a strong network at the workplace:

Be Proactive

Don't wait for others to approach you. Take the initiative to introduce yourself to colleagues and get to know them. Look for opportunities to collaborate on projects or initiatives and volunteer for new responsibilities.

Attend Company Events

Attend company events such as social gatherings, team-building activities, and training sessions. These events provide an opportunity to meet colleagues from different departments and build relationships outside of the workplace.

Join Employee Resource Groups

Many workplaces have employee resource groups that bring together employees with shared interests or backgrounds. Joining these groups can help you connect with others who share your interests and goals.

Offer Help And Support

Be willing to offer help and support to your colleagues. Offer to mentor new hires, share your expertise on a project, or assist a colleague struggling with a task.

Maintain Relationships

Building a strong network requires ongoing effort. Be sure to maintain relationships with your colleagues by checking in regularly, offering congratulations on achievements, and staying in touch after you, or they leave the company.

Overall, building a strong network at the workplace requires being proactive, attending events, joining employee resource groups, offering help and support, and maintaining relationships. By investing in your workplace network, you can gain new opportunities, insights, and bits of knowledge and build strong and long-lasting relationships to help you achieve your career goals.

CHAPTER FIFTEEN

GOOD CHARACTER

Good characteristics, such as honesty, integrity, kindness, and perseverance, are essential for success because they build trust, earn respect, and create positive relationships with others.

Why Is Good Character Important To Success?

Good character is essential for success in both personal and professional life. Here are some reasons why having good character is important to success:

Builds Trust And Credibility

People with good character are more likely to be trusted by others. They have a reputation for being honest, reliable, and dependable, which can help them build strong, positive relationships with others.

Earns Respect

Others respect people with good character. They are seen as role models who set a positive example for others. This can lead to opportunities for leadership and advancement in both personal and professional life.

Enhances Relationships

Good character helps to build positive, healthy relationships with others. People with good character are likelier to be kind, empathetic, and compassionate, which can lead to deeper connections with others.

Increases Resilience

People with good character tend to be more resilient in facing challenges and setbacks. They are likelier to persevere through difficult times and bounce back from failure.

Promotes Success

People with good character are more likely to be successful in their personal and professional lives. They are more likely to be trusted with important responsibilities, earn promotions and other advancement opportunities, and achieve their goals.

Overall, having good character is essential for success because it builds trust, earns respect, enhances relationships, increases resilience, and promotes success. By developing good character traits such as honesty, integrity, kindness, and perseverance, individuals can improve their chances of success in their personal and professional lives.

How To Build A Strong Character?

Building a strong character is a lifelong process that requires intentional effort and commitment. Here are some key strategies for building a strong character:

Define Your Values

Start by defining your values. What is most important to you? What do you stand for? Your values serve as a foundation for your character and guide your decisions and actions.

Practice Self-Awareness

To build a strong character, you must be self-aware. Take time to reflect on your thoughts, feelings, and behaviors. Identify areas where you need to improve and develop new habits and behaviors that align with your values.

Cultivate Positive Habits

Habits are powerful tools for building a strong character. Cultivate positive habits such as kindness, gratitude, honesty, and resilience. Practice these habits daily until they become second nature.

Seek Feedback

Seek feedback from others on your character. Ask for honest feedback from people you trust and respect. Listen to their feedback with an open mind and use it to guide your growth and development.

Embrace Challenges

Building a strong character requires facing challenges and overcoming obstacles. Embrace challenges as opportunities for growth and learning. Use your challenges as opportunities to practice your character strengths and build resilience.

Surround Yourself With Positive Influences

Surround yourself with people who share your values and support your growth and development. Avoid negative influences that may distract you from your values and character strengths.

Overall, building a strong character requires intentional effort and commitment. By defining your values, practicing self-awareness, cultivating positive habits, seeking feedback, embracing challenges, and surrounding yourself with positive influences, you can build a strong character that will serve as a foundation for success in all areas of life.

The Importance Of Good Character In The Workplace

Good character is essential in the workplace because it helps to build trust, foster positive relationships, and promote a healthy and productive work environment.

Here are some reasons why a good character is important in the workplace:

Builds Trust

Trust is essential in the workplace. People with good character are more likely to be trusted by their colleagues and supervisors. This can lead to more opportunities for collaboration, leadership, and advancement.

Enhances Relationships

Good character helps to build positive, healthy relationships with colleagues and supervisors. People with good character are likelier to be kind, empathetic, and respectful. This can lead to better communication, increased productivity, and a more positive work environment.

Promotes Ethical Behavior

People with good character are more likely to behave ethically in the workplace. They are less likely to engage in unethical or illegal behavior, which can lead to legal or financial consequences for the organization.

Increases Job Satisfaction

Good character can lead to increased job satisfaction. People with good character tend to enjoy their work more because they are more likely to be respected and appreciated by their colleagues and supervisors.

Promotes Leadership

Good character is essential for effective leadership. Leaders with good character are more likely to be trusted and respected by their followers. They are more likely to inspire and motivate their followers to achieve their goals.

Overall, good character is important in the workplace because it builds trust, enhances relationships, promotes ethical behavior, increases job satisfaction, and promotes leadership. By developing good character traits such as honesty, integrity, kindness, and respect, individuals can improve their chances of success in the workplace and contribute to a positive and productive work environment.

Good Character Traits You Can Use At Work

Good character traits are essential for success in the workplace. Here are some traits that can help you succeed and thrive in your career:

Honesty

Honesty is a key trait in the workplace. It builds trust, fosters transparency, and promotes ethical behavior. Being honest in all your dealings can help you build strong relationships with colleagues and supervisors and enhance your reputation as a trustworthy and reliable employee.

Integrity

Integrity is closely related to honesty. It involves doing the right thing, even when no one is watching. People with integrity are committed to ethical behavior and hold themselves accountable for their actions. This trait can help you earn respect and trust of your colleagues and supervisors.

Respect

Respect involves treating others with dignity and kindness. It involves recognizing the value and worth of every person and treating them with fairness and consideration. Demonstrating respect can help you build positive relationships with colleagues and create a positive work environment.

Responsibility

Responsibility involves taking ownership of your actions and being accountable for your decisions. It involves being reliable and trustworthy and fulfilling your obligations to the best of your ability. Demonstrating responsibility can help you earn respect and trust of your colleagues and supervisors.

Empathy

Empathy involves understanding and caring about the feelings and experiences of others. It involves listening attentively, showing compassion, and offering support. Demonstrating empathy can help you build strong relationships with colleagues and foster a positive work environment.

Flexibility

Flexibility involves being adaptable and open to change. It involves being willing to learn new things and take on new challenges. Demonstrating flexibility can help you grow and develop in your career and show your colleagues and supervisors that you are willing to go the extra mile to achieve success.

Positive attitude

A positive attitude involves having an optimistic outlook and a can-do spirit. It involves focusing on solutions rather than problems and being willing to take risks and try new things. A positive attitude can help you stay motivated and inspired in your work and inspire your colleagues to do the same.

Overall, good character traits are essential for success in the workplace. By cultivating traits such as honesty, integrity, respect, responsibility, empathy, flexibility, and a positive attitude, you can build strong relationships with colleagues, earn respect and trust of your supervisors, and create a positive and productive work environment.

CHAPTER SIXTEEN

ENTHUSIASTIC

Enthusiasm is a key to success because it fuels passion, energy, and motivation, which are essential for achieving goals and overcoming challenges. It also attracts positivity and opportunities, which can lead to greater success in both personal and professional life.

Is Enthusiasm The Key To Success?

Enthusiasm is often considered to be a key factor in achieving success. When you enthusiastically approach your work, you feel a sense of passion and excitement that can motivate you to achieve your goals and overcome obstacles.

Enthusiasm can be particularly beneficial in the workplace, where it can help you to stand out as an engaged and motivated employee. When you approach your work enthusiastically, you are more likely to produce high-quality work and be willing to go above and beyond your responsibilities. Your positive attitude and energy can also inspire others and help create a positive and productive work environment.

Enthusiasm can also be a key factor in achieving personal success. When you enthusiastically approach your goals, you are more likely to stay motivated and persistent in pursuing them. This can help you overcome challenges and setbacks and ultimately achieve your desired success.

However, enthusiasm alone may not be enough to guarantee success. It is important to have a clear vision of what you want to achieve and a plan for how to get there. Enthusiasm can help you stay motivated and committed to your goals, but you must also take action and make concrete steps toward achieving them.

Additionally, enthusiasm should be balanced with other important traits, such as hard work, discipline, and patience. While enthusiasm can fuel your motivation and energy, it is also important to have the perseverance and focus to see your goals through to completion.

In summary, enthusiasm can be a key factor in achieving success. It can help you stay motivated, inspired, and engaged in pursuing your goals, both in your personal and professional life. However, enthusiasm alone is not enough to guarantee success. It needs to be paired with clear goals, a plan of action, and other important traits, such as hard work and discipline to achieve success over the long term.

How Can Enthusiasm Help You Reach Your Goals?

Enthusiasm can play a crucial role in helping you reach your goals. When you enthusiastically approach your goals, you are more likely to stay motivated and committed to achieving them.

Here are some ways that enthusiasm can help you reach your goals:

Provides Energy And Motivation

Enthusiasm can give you the energy and motivation to take action toward your goals. It can help you overcome procrastination and stay focused on your tasks.

Creates A Positive Mindset

When you enthusiastically approach your goals, you create a positive mindset that can help you overcome setbacks and challenges. A positive attitude can help you stay resilient and persistent in pursuing your goals.

Increases Creativity

Enthusiasm can increase your creativity and problem-solving abilities. When you are enthusiastic about something, you are more likely to think outside the box and come up with new and innovative solutions.

Inspires Others

Your enthusiasm can inspire others around you to get involved and support your goals. When people see how passionate and committed you are, they are likelier to want to be a part of your success.

Helps You Enjoy The Journey

When you enthusiastically approach your goals, you are more likely to enjoy the journey toward achieving them. This can help you stay motivated and committed over the long term.

However, it is important to note that enthusiasm alone is not enough to reach your goals. You must also have a clear action plan and be willing to put in the hard work and discipline required to achieve your goals. Enthusiasm can be a powerful tool to help you stay motivated and focused, but it needs to be combined with other important traits like persistence, patience, and dedication.

In summary, enthusiasm can be a powerful force to help you reach your goals. It provides you with the energy, motivation, and positive mindset needed to overcome obstacles and stay committed over the long term. By approaching your goals with enthusiasm, you can inspire others, increase your creativity, and enjoy the journey toward achieving your dreams.

Why Is Enthusiasm Important In Leadership?

Enthusiasm is an essential quality for effective leadership. When a leader approaches their role with enthusiasm, they inspire their team to be motivated, engaged, and committed to achieving the organization's goals.

Here are some reasons why enthusiasm is important in leadership:

Inspires Others

A leader's enthusiasm can be contagious. They can inspire their team members to be equally enthusiastic and engaged when excited about a project or idea. This can lead to a more productive and energized team.

Builds Morale

Enthusiastic leaders create a positive work environment. When team members see that their leader is passionate and committed, it can boost morale and create a sense of camaraderie among the team.

Encourages Creativity

Enthusiasm can encourage creativity and innovation. When a leader is excited about a new idea, they can inspire their team to think creatively and develop new solutions to problems.

Increases Productivity

When enthusiastic leader leads a team, they are more likely to be motivated and productive. This can lead to better results, higher quality work, and increased efficiency.

Improves Communication

Enthusiastic leaders are more likely to be effective communicators. They are passionate about their vision and can inspire their team members to share their enthusiasm. This can lead to better communication and collaboration among team members.

Fosters A Positive Culture

Enthusiasm can help create a positive and inclusive culture within an organization. When leaders are enthusiastic, they can create a culture where team members feel valued, appreciated, and supported.

In summary, enthusiasm is an important trait for effective leadership. It can inspire and motivate team members, boost morale, encourage creativity, increase productivity, improve communication, and foster a positive culture. When leaders approach their role enthusiastically, they can create a dynamic team committed to achieving the organization's goals.

Why Is Enthusiasm Important In The Workplace?

Enthusiasm is important in the workplace because it can create a positive and productive environment. When employees are enthusiastic about their work, they are more engaged, motivated, and committed to achieving their goals.

Here are some reasons why enthusiasm is important in the workplace:

Increases Motivation

Enthusiasm can boost employee motivation, making them more committed to their work and willing to put in extra effort to achieve their goals. This can lead to higher productivity and better results.

Improves Job Satisfaction

When employees are enthusiastic about their work, they are more likely to feel satisfied and fulfilled. This can lead to higher levels of job satisfaction and lower turnover rates.

Encourages Teamwork

Enthusiasm can encourage teamwork and collaboration. When employees are excited about their work, they are more likely to work together and share ideas to achieve their goals.

Boosts Morale

Enthusiasm can create a positive work environment and boost morale. When employees feel that their work is valued and important, it can lead to a sense of pride and satisfaction in their work.

Inspires Creativity

Enthusiasm can inspire creativity and innovation. When employees are excited about their work, they are more likely to think creatively and develop new solutions to problems.

Enhances Customer Service

Enthusiasm can enhance customer service. When employees are enthusiastic and passionate about their work, they are more likely to provide excellent customer service, increasing customer satisfaction and loyalty.

In summary, enthusiasm is important in the workplace because it can increase motivation, improve job satisfaction, encourage teamwork, boost morale, inspire creativity, and enhance customer service. When employees are enthusiastic about their work, it can create a positive and productive environment, leading to better results and higher levels of success for the organization.

How To Be More Enthusiastic At Work?

Being enthusiastic at work is a great way to increase productivity, improve job satisfaction, and positively impact coworkers and the organization.

Here are some tips on how to be more enthusiastic at work:

Focus On Your Strengths

Identify your strengths and passions, and focus on tasks that align with them. When you enjoy what you do, you are more likely to be enthusiastic and motivated.

Set Goals

Setting clear goals can give you something to work towards and help you stay focused and motivated. Celebrate your accomplishments along the way to maintain enthusiasm and momentum.

Stay Positive

Choose to focus on the positive aspects of your job and your coworkers. Avoid negative talk and complaining, and instead, look for opportunities to learn and grow.

Embrace Challenges

Instead of avoiding difficult tasks or projects, embrace them as opportunities to learn and grow. When you overcome a challenge, it can be a source of pride and enthusiasm.

Take Breaks

Regular breaks can help you recharge and maintain your enthusiasm throughout the day. Use your breaks to do something you enjoy or take a walk to clear your mind.

Learn New Skills

Learning and developing new skills can help you stay engaged and enthusiastic about your work. Seek opportunities for professional development or take on new responsibilities that challenge you.

Celebrate Successes

Celebrate your successes and those of your coworkers. Recognize and acknowledge their achievements, and use them as motivation to keep pushing towards your goals.

Find Meaning In Your Work

Connect your work to a larger purpose or mission, and remind yourself of your impact on others. This can help you find meaning in your work and maintain enthusiasm and motivation.

Stay Organized

Being organized can help you stay on top of your work and avoid feeling overwhelmed or stressed. Create to-do lists, prioritize your tasks, and break larger projects into smaller, more manageable steps.

Surround Yourself With Positivity

Surround yourself with coworkers who are positive, supportive, and enthusiastic. Their energy can be contagious and help you stay motivated and enthusiastic.

In summary, being more enthusiastic at work requires focusing on your strengths, setting goals, staying positive, embracing challenges, taking breaks, learning new skills, celebrating successes, finding meaning in your work, staying organized, and surrounding yourself with positivity. Following these tips can increase your enthusiasm and positively impact your work and those around you.

CHAPTER SEVENTEEN

ADMIT MISTAKES

Admitting and learning from mistakes is crucial for success. To do so, one must acknowledge the mistake, reflect on what went wrong, and take corrective action to prevent it from happening again.

Why Is Admitting Mistakes Important?

Admitting mistakes is an essential aspect of personal and professional growth. It requires confronting their flaws and weaknesses, which can be difficult and uncomfortable. However, admitting mistakes is crucial for several reasons.

Firstly, admitting mistakes is a sign of honesty and integrity. When someone acknowledges their errors, they demonstrate that they are willing to be accountable for their actions. This trait is highly valued in both personal and professional settings. It shows that an individual can be trusted and relied upon to act with integrity.

Secondly, admitting mistakes helps to build trust and strengthen relationships. When someone admits to their mistakes, they are willing to listen to others' perspectives and acknowledge their limitations. This can help foster open communication and understanding between people, which is essential for building positive relationships.

Thirdly, admitting mistakes allows individuals to learn and grow. When someone acknowledges their errors, they can reflect on what went wrong and identify ways to improve in the future. This is a crucial aspect of personal and professional development. It enables individuals to learn from their mistakes and develop the skills and knowledge necessary to succeed.

Finally, admitting mistakes is crucial for effective problem-solving. When someone takes ownership of their mistakes, they can work collaboratively with others to solve the problem. This can help create a continuous improvement and innovation culture, where mistakes are seen as opportunities to learn and grow.

In conclusion, admitting mistakes is essential to personal and professional growth. It requires courage, honesty, and integrity, but it is crucial for building trust, strengthening relationships, learning and growing, and effective problem-solving. By acknowledging their mistakes and taking corrective action, individuals can develop the skills and knowledge necessary to succeed personally and professionally.

How Is Correcting A Mistake Important For Success?

Correcting mistakes is crucial for achieving success in both personal and professional settings. It involves taking responsibility for one's actions, identifying the source of the mistake, and taking corrective action to prevent it from happening again. Correcting mistakes is essential for several reasons.

Firstly, correcting mistakes demonstrates accountability and responsibility. When someone takes ownership of their mistakes and works to correct them, they show that they are responsible for their actions. This trait is highly valued in personal and professional settings as it shows that an individual can be relied upon to act with integrity and professionalism.

Secondly, correcting mistakes can help to prevent future problems. When someone takes the time to identify the source of their mistake, they can implement corrective actions to prevent it from happening again. This can help create a continuous improvement culture, where mistakes are seen as opportunities to learn and grow.

Thirdly, correcting mistakes can help to build trust and strengthen relationships. When someone takes corrective action to address their mistakes, it shows that they are willing to take responsibility for their actions and work collaboratively with others to find solutions to the problem. This can help foster open communication and understanding between people, which is essential for building positive relationships.

Fourthly, correcting mistakes can lead to personal and professional growth. When someone takes the time to reflect on their mistakes and identify areas for improvement, they can develop the skills and knowledge necessary to succeed. This can help build confidence and resilience, which are essential for success in both personal and professional settings.

In conclusion, correcting mistakes is essential for success in both personal and professional settings. It involves taking responsibility for one's actions, identifying the source of the mistake, and taking corrective action to prevent it from happening again. By doing so, individuals can demonstrate accountability and responsibility, prevent future problems, build trust and strengthen relationships, and achieve personal and professional growth.

Good Leaders Admit And Learn From Mistakes

Good leaders acknowledge their mistakes and take responsibility for their actions. They understand that making mistakes is a natural part of learning and use them as opportunities to learn and grow. Good leaders recognize that admitting and learning from mistakes is essential for personal and professional development.

When leaders admit their mistakes, they demonstrate humility and vulnerability. They show that they are willing to learn from their mistakes and take corrective action to prevent them from happening again. This trait builds trust and credibility with the team and creates a culture of open communication and continuous improvement.

Learning from mistakes is crucial for effective leadership. When leaders take the time to reflect on their mistakes and identify areas for improvement, they can develop the skills and knowledge necessary to succeed. This can help them make better future decisions and lead their team with confidence and clarity.

Furthermore, leaders who admit and learn from their mistakes set an example for their team. They create a culture of accountability and responsibility, where mistakes are seen as opportunities to learn and grow. This can help to foster a positive and productive work environment where team members feel valued and supported.

In conclusion, good leaders admit and learn from their mistakes. They understand that making mistakes is a natural part of the learning process and use them as opportunities to improve. By doing so, they build trust and credibility with their team, develop the skills and knowledge necessary to succeed and create a culture of accountability and responsibility.

How To Take Responsibility For A Mistake At Work?

Taking responsibility for a mistake at work is essential to being a professional. It shows integrity, accountability, and personal and professional growth commitment.

Here are some steps to take when taking responsibility for a mistake at work:

Admit The Mistake

The first step is to admit the mistake. Be honest and straightforward in your communication, and avoid making excuses or blaming others.

Apologize

Take responsibility for the mistake and apologize to anyone affected by it. This demonstrates that you are taking the situation seriously and committed to making it right.

Identify The Cause

Take the time to identify the cause of the mistake. This can help you to understand what went wrong and prevent similar mistakes from happening in the future.

Take Corrective Action

Once you have identified the cause of the mistake, take corrective action to prevent it from happening again. This could involve implementing new procedures, seeking additional training or support, or making changes to your approach.

Learn From The Mistake

Use the experience as an opportunity to learn and grow. Reflect on what went wrong and what you could do differently in the future.

In conclusion, taking responsibility for a mistake at work is essential for personal and professional growth. By admitting the mistake, apologizing, identifying the cause, taking corrective action, and learning from the experience, you can demonstrate integrity, accountability, and a commitment to continuous improvement.

CHAPTER EIGHTEEN

ENERGY CONSCIOUS

Effective energy management is crucial for success at work. It involves taking breaks, staying hydrated, getting enough sleep, and focusing on one task at a time, which can help you to maintain focus, productivity, and motivation throughout the day.

Why Is Energy Important For Success?

Managing energy is essential for achieving success in both personal and professional settings. Energy management involves maintaining a balance between physical, emotional, and mental energy levels, which can significantly impact one's ability to be productive, engaged, and effective.

Here are some reasons why managing energy is important for success:

Increases Productivity

When energy levels are high, productivity levels also tend to be higher. Managing energy can help individuals maintain focus, motivation, and engagement, leading to greater productivity and success.

Improves Decision-Making

High energy levels can help individuals to make better decisions, think more creatively, and approach problems with greater clarity and objectivity. By managing energy effectively, individuals can improve their ability to make sound decisions and achieve success.

Boosts Resilience

Managing energy can also help individuals to build resilience and overcome challenges more effectively. By maintaining a balance between physical, emotional, and mental energy levels, individuals can improve their ability to cope with stress, uncertainty, and adversity, which are common in both personal and professional settings.

Increases Satisfaction

When energy levels are high, individuals feel more satisfied and fulfilled with their work and personal lives. Effective energy management can help individuals achieve balance and well-being, contributing to greater satisfaction and success.

Promotes Longevity

Finally, managing energy can contribute to a longer and healthier life. By maintaining a balance between physical, emotional, and mental energy levels, individuals can reduce the risk of burnout, chronic stress, and other health problems that can impact longevity and quality of life.

In conclusion, managing energy is critical for success in both personal and professional settings. By balancing physical, emotional, and mental energy levels, individuals can increase productivity, improve decision-making, boost resilience, increase satisfaction, and promote longevity. Effective energy management can help individuals to achieve success, fulfillment, and well-being in all areas of their lives.

Why Do Successful People Have High Levels Of Energy?

Successful people often have high energy levels because they understand the importance of balancing physical, emotional, and mental energy levels. They recognize that high energy levels can increase productivity, creativity, and engagement, leading to greater success.

Furthermore, successful people often prioritize self-care and energy management strategies, such as regular exercise, healthy eating habits, and stress-reducing activities. They understand that taking care of their physical health can improve their mental and emotional well-being, contributing to higher energy levels.

Additionally, successful people often have a clear sense of purpose and passion for their work, which can fuel their energy levels and motivation. When individuals are passionate about their work and committed to their goals, they are likelier to experience high energy and engagement.

Successful people also tend to be highly disciplined and focused, which can contribute to their ability to manage their energy effectively. They prioritize their time and activities to align with their goals and values, which can help them avoid burnout and maintain a consistent energy level.

In conclusion, successful people often have high energy levels because they prioritize energy management strategies, have a clear sense of purpose and passion for their work, and are disciplined and focused. By maintaining a balance between physical, emotional, and mental energy levels, individuals can increase their productivity, creativity, and engagement, contributing to greater success in all areas of their lives.

How To Activate Your Energy For Success?

Activating your energy for success requires intentional effort and attention. Here are some strategies to help you activate your energy for success:

Exercise Regularly

Regular physical activity can increase your energy levels and improve your overall well-being. Aim for at least 30 minutes of moderate daily exercise, such as walking, jogging, or cycling.

Prioritize Sleep

Getting enough sleep is essential for maintaining high energy levels. Aim for 7-8 hours of sleep per night and establish a consistent sleep routine.

Stay Hydrated

Dehydration can lead to fatigue and decreased energy levels. Make sure to drink plenty of water throughout the day.

Eat A Healthy Diet

A healthy diet can give you the nutrients and energy needed to succeed. Focus on eating whole foods, including fruits, vegetables, lean proteins, and whole grains.

Manage Stress

Chronic stress can drain your energy levels and impact your overall health. Develop strategies to manage stress, such as meditation, deep breathing exercises, or yoga.

Pursue Your Passions

Engage in activities that you enjoy and that align with your values and goals. Pursuing your passions can increase your motivation and energy levels.

Surround Yourself With Positive People

Negative people can drain your energy and impact your overall well-being. Surround yourself with positive, supportive people who inspire and motivate you.

In conclusion, activating your energy for success requires intentional effort and attention. Incorporating these strategies into your daily routine can increase your energy levels and overall well-being, contributing to greater success in all areas of your life.

How To Manage Your Energy More Effectively At Work?

Managing your energy effectively at work is essential for maintaining high productivity and achieving your goals. Here are some strategies to help you manage your energy more effectively at work:

Prioritize Your Most Important Tasks

Start your day by prioritizing your most important tasks and focusing on completing them first. This can help you to maintain a sense of accomplishment and motivation throughout the day.

Take Breaks

Taking short breaks throughout the day can help you to recharge your energy levels and reduce stress. Take a quick walk, stretch, or meditate to help clear your mind and refocus.

Manage Your Time Effectively

Managing your time effectively can help you to avoid feeling overwhelmed and stressed. Use time management strategies such as setting deadlines, breaking down large projects into smaller tasks, and utilizing productivity tools like calendars and task lists.

Learn To Say No

Saying yes to everything can lead to overcommitment and burnout. Learn to say no to requests that do not align with your goals or values.

Practice Good Sleep Hygiene

Getting enough quality sleep is essential for maintaining high energy levels. Establish a consistent sleep routine and avoid using electronic devices before bedtime.

Stay Hydrated

Dehydration can lead to fatigue and decreased energy levels. Keep a water bottle at your desk and drink water throughout the day.

Surround Yourself With Positive People

Surrounding yourself with positive, supportive colleagues can increase your motivation and energy levels. Seek mentors or colleagues who inspire and motivate you.

In conclusion, managing your energy effectively at work requires intentional effort and attention. By incorporating these strategies into your daily routine, you can increase productivity, reduce stress, and achieve your goals more effectively.

CHAPTER NINETEEN

SELF RELIANT

Self-reliance is crucial for success as it helps individuals take ownership of their actions and decisions, leading to greater accountability and responsibility. Additionally, self-reliance enables individuals to build resilience and adaptability, key traits for success in an ever-changing world.

Is Self-Reliance A Good Thing?

Self-reliance is generally considered a good thing as it promotes independence and responsibility. It means that individuals can care for themselves and not depend on others to meet their needs. Self-reliant individuals are more likely to be self-sufficient and have greater control over their lives.

Self-reliance also promotes personal growth and development. By taking ownership of their actions and decisions, individuals can learn from their mistakes and grow from their experiences. They can develop problem-solving skills, build resilience, and become more adaptable to change.

However, it is important to note that self-reliance does not mean individuals should never ask for help or support. Seeking help when needed is a sign of strength, not weakness. Additionally, self-reliance should not be confused with isolation or self-sufficiency. Individuals need to cultivate supportive relationships and communities.

In conclusion, self-reliance can be good as it promotes independence, responsibility, personal growth, and development. However, individuals must balance self-reliance with seeking help and cultivating supportive relationships and communities.

How Does Self-Reliance Lead To Success?

Self-reliance is an important trait that can lead to success in various aspects of life.

Here are some ways self-reliance helps lead to success:

Increased Responsibility

Self-reliant individuals take ownership of their actions and decisions, leading to greater responsibility and accountability. This mindset helps individuals to become more reliable and trustworthy, which are important traits for success.

Better Decision-Making

Self-reliant individuals are more confident in their decision-making, which leads to better decision-making. They are unafraid to take risks, make mistakes, and learn from their experiences. This leads to better outcomes and greater control over their lives.

Improved Resilience

Self-reliant individuals are better equipped to handle challenges and setbacks. They are more resilient and adaptable, which helps them bounce back from failures and continue moving toward their goals.

Increased Productivity

Self-reliant individuals can take action and get things done without relying on others. This leads to increased productivity and efficiency, which can help them to achieve their goals more quickly and effectively.

Greater Sense of Independence

Self-reliant individuals are not dependent on others for their needs and can rely on themselves. This leads to a greater sense of independence, boosting confidence and self-esteem.

Better Problem-Solving Skills

Self-reliant individuals can think critically and creatively to solve problems. They are not afraid to take on challenges and find innovative solutions to complex problems.

In conclusion, self-reliance can lead to success in various aspects of life. By taking ownership of their actions and decisions, self-reliant individuals become more responsible, make better decisions, improve their resilience, increase their productivity, develop a greater sense of independence, and improve their problem-solving skills. These traits are essential for success, and cultivating self-reliance can help individuals achieve their goals and reach their full potential.

How Self-Reliance Builds Your Self-Confidence?

Self-reliance and self-confidence are closely related, often leading to each other. When individuals take ownership of their actions and decisions, they build their self-reliance, which, in turn, helps to build their self-confidence.

Here are some ways self-reliance helps build self-confidence:

Independence

Self-reliant individuals are not dependent on others for their needs, leading to greater independence. This independence can boost confidence and self-esteem as individuals feel more capable of caring for themselves.

Problem-solving Skills

Self-reliant individuals can think critically and creatively to solve problems. This builds confidence as they become more adept at finding solutions to challenging situations.

Responsibility

Self-reliant individuals take ownership of their actions and decisions, which leads to greater responsibility and accountability. This responsibility can build confidence as individuals become more reliable and trustworthy.

Resilience

Self-reliant individuals are better equipped to handle challenges and setbacks, which builds resilience. This resilience can boost confidence as individuals become more confident in overcoming obstacles and returning from failures.

In conclusion, self-reliance builds self-confidence in various ways. By developing independence, problem-solving skills, responsibility, and resilience, self-reliant individuals become more confident in their abilities and self-assured in their actions and decisions. As a result, they are better able to take on challenges, achieve their goals, and reach their full potential.

How To Develop Self-Reliance?

Self-reliance is an important trait that can help individuals succeed in various aspects of life. Here are some tips on how to develop self-reliance:

Take Ownership Of Your Actions

One of the first steps towards self-reliance is owning your actions and decisions. Instead of blaming others or making excuses, take responsibility for your mistakes and learn from them.

Set Goals And Take Action

Self-reliant individuals set goals for themselves and take action toward achieving them. Identify what you want to achieve and create a plan of action to get there.

Learn To Be Resourceful

Self-reliant individuals learn to be resourceful and find solutions to problems independently. Develop your problem-solving skills and seek new information and resources when facing challenges.

Embrace Independence

Self-reliant individuals are independent and do not rely on others for their needs. Embrace your independence and take steps towards becoming self-sufficient.

Cultivate Resilience

Self-reliant individuals are resilient and able to bounce back from setbacks. Develop your resilience by practicing mindfulness, gratitude, and positive self-talk.

Learn To Manage Your Emotions

Self-reliant individuals can manage their emotions and remain calm in difficult situations. Practice mindfulness and develop techniques to help you manage stress and anxiety.

Seek Out New Experiences

Self-reliant individuals seek new experiences and challenges to help them grow and learn. Try new things, take on new responsibilities, and step out of your comfort zone.

In conclusion, developing self-reliance takes time and effort, but the benefits are well worth it.

CHAPTER TWENTY

SELF CONTROL

Self-control is an important factor that leads to success. It allows individuals to make better decisions, avoid distractions, and focus on their goals.

How Does Self-Control Lead To Success?

Self-control, also known as self-discipline, regulates one's emotions, thoughts, and behaviors to achieve a desired outcome. It is an important trait that can help individuals succeed in various aspects of life.

Here are some ways how self-control leads to success:

Better Decision-Making

Self-control allows individuals to make better decisions. When faced with a difficult decision, individuals with self-control can weigh the pros and cons, consider the consequences of their actions, and make a well-informed choice. This can help them avoid impulsive decisions that may lead to adverse outcomes.

Increased Productivity

Self-control also leads to increased productivity. Individuals with self-control can avoid distractions and stay focused on their goals. They can prioritize their tasks and use their time more efficiently, leading to greater productivity.

Improved Relationships

Self-control can also improve relationships. When individuals can regulate their emotions and behavior, they are less likely to lash out or act impulsively. This can lead to more positive interactions and better relationships with others.

Greater Financial Stability

Self-control can also lead to excellent financial stability. Individuals with self-control can resist the temptation to overspend or make impulsive purchases. They can set financial goals and stick to a budget, leading to greater financial security.

Improved Health

Self-control can also lead to improved health. Individuals with self-control can make healthier choices regarding diet, exercise, and lifestyle habits. They are less likely to engage in unhealthy behaviors such as smoking, overeating, or drinking too much alcohol.

Greater Self-Confidence

Self-control can also lead to greater self-confidence. When individuals can regulate their emotions and behavior, they feel more in control of their lives. This can lead to greater self-confidence and a sense of personal empowerment.

In conclusion, self-control is an important trait that can lead to success in various aspects of life. By improving decision-making, increasing productivity, improving relationships, achieving greater financial stability, improving health, and increasing self-confidence, self-control can help individuals achieve their goals and reach their full potential.

Why Is Self-Control Important In The Workplace?

Self-control is crucial in many aspects of life, including the workplace. Here are some reasons why self-control is important in the workplace:

Better Decision-Making

Employees often face difficult decisions in the workplace that can have significant consequences. Self-control allows employees to make better decisions by considering all available information and avoiding impulsive or emotional reactions.

Improved Work Performance

Self-control can also lead to improved work performance. Employees can complete their work more efficiently and effectively by staying focused and avoiding distractions. They can also prioritize their tasks and manage their time more effectively, leading to better outcomes.

Stronger Relationships With Colleagues

Self-control can also improve relationships with colleagues. Employees can create a more positive and collaborative work environment by regulating emotions and avoiding emotional outbursts or conflicts. This can lead to stronger relationships with colleagues, improved teamwork, and better outcomes.

Improved Stress Management

The workplace can be stressful, and self-control is important for managing stress. Employees can better manage stressful situations and maintain a positive outlook by staying calm and focused.

Greater Career Success

Finally, self-control is important for achieving tremendous career success. By making better decisions, improving work performance, building strong relationships with colleagues, and managing stress effectively, employees are better positioned for career advancement and success.

Overall, self-control is an important skill for success in the workplace. By improving decision-making, work performance, relationships with colleagues, stress management, and career success, self-control can help employees achieve their goals and reach their full potential.

How To Build And Improve Your Self-Control?

Building and improving self-control can be challenging, but it is a worthwhile endeavor that can lead to success in many areas of life, including the workplace.

Here are some strategies for building and improving your self-control:

Identify Triggers

The first step in building self-control is identifying what triggers you to lose control. This could be a particular person, situation, or emotion. Once you have identified your triggers, you can work on developing strategies for managing them.

Practice Mindfulness

Mindfulness is a powerful tool for building self-control. By practicing mindfulness, you can become more aware of your thoughts and emotions and learn to manage them more effectively. Mindfulness can also help you stay focused and avoid distractions.

Exercise Regularly

Regular exercise has been shown to improve self-control. Exercise releases endorphins, improving mood and reducing stress, making it easier to regulate emotions and stay focused.

Get Enough Sleep

Getting enough sleep is crucial for self-control. Lack of sleep can make regulating emotions and good decisions more difficult. Aim for seven to nine hours of sleep each night.

Set Goals

Setting goals can help you stay focused and motivated. When setting goals, make sure they are specific, measurable, achievable, relevant, and time-bound (SMART). Having a clear goal can help you stay on track and avoid distractions.

Practice Self-Care

Taking care of yourself is important for building self-control. This includes eating a healthy diet, drinking plenty of water, and taking breaks when needed. Taking care of your physical health can help you stay focused and avoid distractions.

Use Positive Self-Talk

Positive self-talk can help you stay motivated and focused. When you struggle to maintain self-control, try using positive affirmations to stay on track.

Practice Delayed Gratification

Delayed gratification is a key component of self-control. This means delaying immediate rewards for long-term goals. For example, instead of indulging in a tempting treat, choose a healthier option to help you achieve your long-term health goals.

Seek Support

Building self-control can be challenging, and it's important to have support from others. Seek out friends, family members, or colleagues who can offer encouragement and support as you work to build your self-control.

Building and improving self-control takes time and effort, but it is a worthwhile investment in your personal and professional success. By identifying triggers, practicing mindfulness, exercising regularly, getting enough sleep, setting goals, practicing self-care, using positive self-talk, practicing delayed gratification, and seeking support, you can build your self-control and achieve your goals.

CHAPTER TWENTY-ONE

SELF ESTEEM

High self-esteem is important for success because it helps individuals believe in themselves and their abilities, increasing motivation and confidence in pursuing their goals. Conversely, low self-esteem can hinder success by causing individuals to doubt themselves and their capabilities.

Why Is High Self-Esteem So Important To Success?

Self-esteem refers to the belief and confidence one has in their worth and abilities. It plays a critical role in an individual's overall mental and emotional well-being and is also a key factor in determining success.

Here are some reasons why high self-esteem is so important to success:

Increased Confidence

High self-esteem leads to increased confidence in oneself and one's abilities. This confidence can translate into taking more risks, pursuing more challenging goals, and not being afraid to step out of one's comfort zone. This can lead to more opportunities and, ultimately, more success.

Resilience

Individuals with high self-esteem are more resilient when faced with obstacles and setbacks. They can better bounce back from failures and mistakes and use them as learning opportunities. This resilience is essential for success, as setbacks are inevitable on the road to achieving one's goals.

Better Decision-Making

Individuals with high self-esteem tend to make better decisions, as they are not as easily influenced by the opinions of others. They trust their judgment and are confident in making the right choices.

More Motivation

High self-esteem leads to more motivation to succeed. When individuals believe in themselves and their abilities, they are more likely to set ambitious goals and work hard to achieve them.

Improved Relationships

High self-esteem can also lead to improved relationships with others. Individuals with high self-esteem tend to be more confident and assertive, which can help them establish healthier boundaries and communicate more effectively with others.

Increased Happiness

Finally, high self-esteem is associated with increased happiness and life satisfaction. When individuals feel good about themselves, they are more likely to enjoy life and experience positive emotions.

Overall, high self-esteem is essential for success in all areas of life. It leads to increased confidence, resilience, better decision-making, more motivation, improved relationships, and increased happiness. While building self-esteem is a lifelong process, it can be improved with practice and self-reflection.

How To Have High Self-Esteem?

High self-esteem is essential for success and well-being in all areas of life. Here are some tips on how to build and maintain high self-esteem:

Practice Self-Compassion

Treat yourself with kindness and compassion. When you make a mistake, avoid self-blame and negative self-talk. Instead, practice self-compassion by speaking to yourself as you would to a friend.

Focus On Your Strengths

Recognize and celebrate your strengths, skills, and accomplishments. List your positive qualities and achievements and refer to them often.

Challenge Negative Self-Talk

Pay attention to your inner dialogue and challenge negative self-talk when it arises. Replace negative thoughts with positive affirmations.

Set Realistic Goals

Set goals that are realistic and achievable. Celebrate small accomplishments and use them as motivation to keep going.

Practice Self-Care

Take care of yourself physically, mentally, and emotionally. Exercise regularly, eat a healthy diet, get enough sleep, and practice stress-reduction techniques like meditation or yoga.

Surround Yourself With Positivity

Surround yourself with positive and supportive people who uplift and encourage you to be your best self.

Learn To Say No

Set boundaries and learn to say no to things that don't align with your values or goals. This will help you prioritize what's important and reduce stress and overwhelm.

Take Action

Don't let fear or self-doubt stop you from taking action toward your goals. Take small daily steps towards your goals, and celebrate your progress.

You can build and maintain high self-esteem by practicing self-compassion, focusing on your strengths, challenging negative self-talk, setting realistic goals, practicing self-care, surrounding yourself with positivity, learning to say no, and taking action. This will help you achieve success and well-being in all areas of your life.

How Important Is Self-Esteem In The Workplace?

Self-esteem is a crucial factor for success in the workplace. Individuals with high self-esteem have greater confidence, resilience, and motivation to achieve their goals.

Here are some reasons why self-esteem is important in the workplace:

Improved Performance

People with high self-esteem are likelier to perform well at work as they believe in their abilities and are confident in their skills. They take on challenges with a positive attitude, are motivated to learn and grow, and are more likely to take risks, which can lead to innovation and creativity.

Better Relationships

Individuals with high self-esteem have a positive outlook and are likelier to build healthy relationships with their colleagues, clients, and customers. They are more approachable, have better communication skills, and are more open to feedback, which can improve collaboration and teamwork.

Increased Resilience

People with high self-esteem are better equipped to handle stress and setbacks in the workplace. They are more resilient and can bounce back from failures and mistakes. This enables them to stay focused on their goals, remain positive, and persevere through difficult times.

Career Advancement

Self-esteem plays a crucial role in career advancement. Individuals with high self-esteem tend to take on leadership roles, seek growth opportunities, and negotiate better pay and benefits. They are confident in their abilities and are not afraid to advocate for themselves, which can lead to tremendous success and advancement in their careers.

Positive Workplace Culture

The attitudes and behaviors of employees greatly influence workplace culture. Individuals with high self-esteem can create a positive workplace culture by modeling positive attitudes, behaviors, and communication styles. This can lead to a more supportive and collaborative work environment, improving job satisfaction and employee retention.

In summary, self-esteem is a critical factor in the workplace, impacting performance, relationships, resilience, career advancement, and workplace culture. Individuals can achieve greater success and well-being in their careers by building and maintaining high self-esteem.

CHAPTER TWENTY-TWO

GREAT COMPANY

Surrounding yourself with good people is crucial for success because they can provide support, encouragement, and valuable feedback. Good people can also serve as role models and help you develop positive habits and attitudes that contribute to your success.

Why Surrounding Yourself With Good People Is Important?

The people we surround ourselves with can significantly impact our lives, particularly when achieving success. Surrounding yourself with good people is important because they can provide many benefits that contribute to your overall well-being and success.

Firstly, good people can offer support and encouragement. When faced with challenges or setbacks, it is natural to feel discouraged or overwhelmed. However, having supportive people around us can make all the difference. They can provide a listening ear, offer wisdom or encouragement, and help us navigate difficult situations. This support can be invaluable, especially when striving towards a challenging goal or pursuing a new opportunity.

Secondly, good people can offer valuable feedback. Sometimes, we become so focused on our perspectives and ideas that we fail to see potential blind spots or areas for improvement. However, good people can offer constructive criticism and feedback to help us grow and develop. By listening to feedback from those we trust and respect, we can gain new insights, improve our skills, and become more effective.

Thirdly, good people can serve as role models. We are likelier to adopt similar qualities when we surround ourselves with successful, motivated, and positive people. These individuals can inspire us to set high goals, work hard, and maintain a positive attitude. By observing their habits and behaviors, we can learn valuable lessons that can help us achieve success in our own lives.

Finally, good people can help us develop positive habits and attitudes. When we spend time with people who are kind, generous, and optimistic, we are more likely to adopt similar qualities. We can learn to be more patient, empathetic, and understanding by cultivating positive relationships. These qualities can contribute to our well-being and success in relationships, careers, and other areas of life.

In conclusion, surrounding ourselves with good people is critical for achieving success. They can offer support, feedback, and inspiration while helping us develop positive habits and attitudes. By investing in relationships with positive and supportive individuals, we can create a network of people who can help us achieve our goals and lead fulfilling lives.

How Do You Decide Who Gets To Be In Your Inner Circle?

Your inner circle is a group of people you trust and rely on for support, advice, and encouragement. These individuals play a crucial role in your life, so it is important to choose them carefully.

Here are some factors to consider when deciding who gets to be in your inner circle:

Shared Values

The people in your inner circle should share your values and beliefs. This ensures that you are surrounded by individuals aligned with your goals and vision for the future. It is important to have people who can challenge you, but ultimately, your inner circle should be made up of individuals who support your values and help you stay true to yourself.

Positive Energy

Your inner circle should be filled with people who radiate positive energy. These individuals should uplift you and help you feel motivated and inspired. Negative people or those who constantly bring you down should be avoided. Surrounding yourself with positive people can help you maintain a positive mindset and outlook, which is essential for success.

Trustworthiness

The people in your inner circle should be trustworthy and reliable. These individuals should have your best interests at heart and be committed to helping you achieve your goals. They should communicate honestly and transparently, and you should feel comfortable sharing your thoughts and feelings with them.

Reciprocity

Your inner circle should comprise individuals who give as much as they take. These individuals should be willing to support you in your endeavors and be there for you when you need them. However, it is also important to reciprocate this support and be there for them when they need you.

Diversity

Your inner circle should be diverse in terms of backgrounds, experiences, and perspectives. This ensures that you are exposed to different viewpoints and ideas, which can help you grow and develop as a person. Diversity can also help you build a stronger network and open new opportunities.

Ultimately, the people in your inner circle should be individuals who bring out the best in you and help you achieve your goals. They should be supportive, trustworthy, and positive while challenging you to grow and develop. By carefully selecting your inner circle, you can create a supportive network to help you navigate life's challenges and succeed.

Why And How To Let Go Of Negative People In Your Life?

Negative people can significantly impact our lives, and it is important to let go of them to create a more positive and fulfilling life.

Here are some reasons why and how to let go of negative people in your life:

Negative People Drain Your Energy

Negative people tend to focus on the negative aspects of life and bring down those around them. They can drain your energy and leave you feeling exhausted and unmotivated. By letting go of negative people, you can create more space for positive and uplifting relationships that energize and help you thrive.

Negative People Can Hold You Back

Negative people can be a hindrance to your personal and professional growth. They may discourage you from pursuing your goals, or they may not support you in your endeavors. By letting go of negative people, you can surround yourself with people who support and encourage your growth and development.

Negative People Can Be Toxic

Some negative people can be toxic and even abusive. They may criticize, belittle, or manipulate you. It is important to recognize when a relationship has become toxic and to let go of it for your well-being and safety.

So, how do you let go of negative people in your life?

Set Boundaries

Start by setting clear boundaries with negative people. Tell them what behaviors are unacceptable and what you are willing and unwilling to tolerate in a relationship. Stick to these boundaries; if they continue to violate them, it may be time to let go.

Communicate Openly

Be honest and direct with negative people about how their behavior affects you. Allow them to make changes, but also be prepared to walk away if they are unwilling or unable to do so.

Surround Yourself With Positive People

Focus on building relationships with people who are positive, uplifting, and supportive. Seek out people who share your values and goals and inspire you to be your best self.

Practice Self-Care

Letting go of negative people can be difficult, so taking care of yourself during the process is important. Engage in activities that bring you joy and fulfillment, and seek support from positive people.

In conclusion, letting go of negative people can be challenging, but it is essential for creating a positive and fulfilling life. By setting boundaries, communicating openly, surrounding yourself with positive people, and practicing self-care, you can let go of negative relationships and create space for positive and uplifting ones.

How To Upgrade Your Social Circle With High-Value People?

Upgrading your social circle with high-value people can significantly impact your personal and professional life. High-value people are individuals who share your values and goals and can offer support, guidance, and opportunities for growth.

Here are some tips on how to upgrade your social circle with high-value people:

Identify Your Values And Goals

Before you can upgrade your social circle, it is important to identify your values and goals. What are your priorities in life, and what do you want to achieve? Once you understand your values and goals clearly, you can seek out people who share them.

Attend Networking Events

Networking events are a great way to meet new people who share your interests and goals. Look for events that are relevant to your industry or hobbies, and make an effort to connect with people who are successful and influential.

Join Professional Organizations

Professional organizations can provide opportunities to meet like-minded people passionate about their work. Look for organizations relevant to your industry, and attend meetings and events regularly to build relationships with other members.

Volunteer

Volunteering is a great way to meet new people and give back to your community. Look for volunteer opportunities that align with your interests and values, and make an effort to connect with other volunteers and organizers.

Take Classes Or Workshops

Classes and workshops provide opportunities to learn new skills and meet new people. Look for classes or workshops relevant to your interests and goals, and try to connect with other students and instructors.

Be Proactive

Upgrading your social circle requires effort and intention. Be proactive about reaching out to people who inspire you, and try to build relationships with them. Be genuine and authentic in your interactions, and offer value in return.

In conclusion, upgrading your social circle with high-value people can significantly impact your life. By identifying your values and goals, attending networking events, joining professional organizations, volunteering, taking classes or workshops, and being proactive, you can build relationships with people who share your interests and goals and who can help you succeed.

CHAPTER TWENTY-THREE

MINDSET OF ABUNDANCE

An abundance mindset is important for success as it helps individuals focus on possibilities and opportunities rather than limitations and scarcity. It enables them to approach challenges with an optimistic outlook and to be open to new ideas and experiences that can lead to success.

What Is The Power Of An Abundance Mindset?

An abundance mindset is a way of thinking that focuses on life's opportunities and possibilities rather than limitations and scarcity. When you have an abundance mindset, you believe there is more than enough to go around and that there are always new opportunities and possibilities.

The power of an abundance mindset lies in its ability to shift your perspective and help you see the world more optimistically. Rather than dwelling on what you don't have, you focus on what you do have and on the potential for growth and success in your life.

An abundance mindset can help you overcome challenges and obstacles with a more positive and resilient attitude. Rather than seeing setbacks as failures, you see them as opportunities to learn and grow and to find new ways to succeed.

With an abundance mindset, you are also more open to new ideas and experiences. Your preconceived notions or beliefs do not limit you, and you are more willing to take risks and try new things.

Ultimately, the power of an abundance mindset lies in its ability to help you create a more fulfilling and successful life. By focusing on abundant opportunities and possibilities, you can attract more positive experiences and achieve tremendous success and happiness.

How Can An Abundance Mindset Set You Up For Success?

An abundance mindset can set you up for success in many ways. When you approach life with an abundance mindset, you focus on your opportunities and possibilities rather than limitations and scarcity.

This mindset can help you achieve success in the following ways:

Greater Resilience

When you have an abundance mindset, you are more resilient in facing challenges and setbacks. You see obstacles as opportunities to learn and grow rather than insurmountable barriers. This resilience can help you overcome obstacles and achieve your goals.

Positive Attitude

An abundance mindset helps you maintain an optimistic attitude. This positivity can help you attract more positive experiences and opportunities. People are naturally drawn to optimistic individuals, which can open doors to new relationships, collaborations, and opportunities.

Creative Thinking

An abundance mindset encourages creative thinking and problem-solving. When you focus on abundance, you are more likely to approach problems with a mindset of possibility rather than limitation. This can help you come up with innovative solutions that lead to success.

Increased Confidence

An abundance mindset can increase your confidence and self-esteem. You are more likely to take risks and confidently pursue your goals when you believe there is enough to go around and opportunities are available. This can lead to greater success in all areas of your life.

Gratitude

An abundance mindset encourages gratitude for what you have rather than focusing on what you don't have. Gratitude has been linked to greater happiness and well-being and can help you maintain a positive outlook on life.

In conclusion, an abundance mindset can set you up for success in many ways. By focusing on the abundance of opportunities and possibilities in your life, you can increase your resilience, maintain a positive attitude, encourage creative thinking, increase your confidence, and cultivate gratitude. These qualities can help you achieve success in all areas of your life, from personal relationships to professional pursuits.

How Do You Go From A Scarcity To An Abundance Mindset?

Going from a scarcity mindset to an abundance mindset requires a shift in your thinking and behavior. Here are some steps you can take to make this transition:

Recognize Your Current Mindset

The first step to shifting from a scarcity to an abundance mindset is to recognize your current mindset. Pay attention to your thoughts and beliefs about the world and yourself. Do you often focus on what you don't have? Are you constantly worried about the future? Once you recognize your current mindset, you can start to work on changing it.

Practice Gratitude

Practicing gratitude is a powerful way to shift from a scarcity to an abundance mindset. Start a gratitude journal and write down three things you're grateful for daily. Focus on what you do have rather than what you don't have. This practice can help you cultivate a more positive outlook on life.

Surround Yourself With Positive People

Surrounding yourself with positive, like-minded individuals can help you shift your mindset. Seek out people who have an abundance mindset and learn from them. Their positivity and optimism can be contagious.

Focus On Possibilities

Instead of focusing on what you don't have, focus on what is possible. Start with small goals and work towards achieving them. Celebrate your successes, and use them as fuel to keep going.

Take Action

An abundance mindset requires action. Take steps towards your goals, even if they are small. Action can help build momentum and confidence and can help you achieve success.

Practice Mindfulness

Mindfulness can help you stay present and focused on the moment rather than worrying about the future or dwelling on the past. This practice can help you cultivate a more positive and abundant mindset.

In conclusion, shifting from a scarcity to an abundance mindset requires consciously changing your thinking and behavior. By practicing gratitude, surrounding yourself with positive people, focusing on possibilities, taking action, and practicing mindfulness, you can cultivate an abundance mindset that can lead to greater success and happiness in your life.

How To Cultivate An Abundance Mindset At Work?

Cultivating an abundance mindset can help you approach your job positively and achieve greater success.

Here are some steps you can take to cultivate an abundance mindset at work:

Focus On Opportunities, Not Limitations

Instead of dwelling on what you can't do or what's not possible, focus on the opportunities available to you. Look for ways to create value and contribute to your team, and don't be afraid to take on new challenges.

Practice Gratitude

Take time each day to appreciate the things that are going well in your work life. Make a list of what you're grateful for, and focus on the positive aspects of your job. This practice can help you stay positive and motivated, even during challenging times.

Celebrate Successes

When you or your team achieve a goal or accomplish something noteworthy, take time to celebrate. This can help build momentum and encourage you to work towards your goals.

Support And Encourage Others

Encouraging and supporting your colleagues can create a positive and supportive work environment. This can lead to greater collaboration and teamwork, which can help you achieve your goals more efficiently.

Take Risks

An abundance mindset encourages risk-taking and experimentation. Don't be afraid to try new things, even if they don't always work out. This can help you learn and grow and can lead to new opportunities.

Learn From Failure

When things don't go as planned, use the experience as an opportunity to learn and grow. Instead of dwelling on your mistakes, look for ways to improve and do better next time.

Be Proactive

An abundance mindset requires action. Take proactive steps towards your goals, even if they are small. This can help build momentum and confidence and can lead to greater success.

In conclusion, cultivating an abundance mindset at work can help you positively approach your job and achieve greater success.

CHAPTER TWENTY-FOUR

WELL BALANCED

Maintaining a balance between work and the rest of your life is crucial for long-term success and happiness. Neglecting personal relationships and self-care can lead to burnout and hinder overall productivity.

Why Is Balance The Key To Success?

Balance is key to success because it allows individuals to achieve their goals and attain success while maintaining their mental and physical well-being. When a person constantly works and neglects other areas of their life, such as personal relationships, hobbies, and self-care, it can lead to burnout, stress, and even health problems.

Maintaining a balance between work and personal life can help individuals avoid burnout and reduce stress. It can also increase productivity as individuals can focus better when not overwhelmed with work-related stress.

Furthermore, maintaining a balance allows individuals to develop a well-rounded life. Pursuing hobbies and spending time with loved ones can give individuals a sense of fulfillment and happiness that can contribute to overall success and satisfaction.

In addition, maintaining a balance allows individuals to prioritize their goals and make time for activities that align with their values and interests. This can lead to greater motivation and purpose, contributing to long-term success.

In conclusion, balance is key to success because it helps individuals achieve their goals while maintaining their well-being, reducing stress, increasing productivity, providing a sense of fulfillment and happiness, and allowing individuals to prioritize their values and interests.

What Are The Benefits Of A Balanced Life?

A balanced life is a state in which an individual can effectively manage and prioritize different aspects of their life, including work, relationships, health, personal growth, and leisure.

Here are some of the benefits of a balanced life:

Reduced Stress

Balancing the various aspects of life can help reduce stress levels. When an individual can effectively manage their responsibilities, they can avoid feelings of overwhelm and burnout.

Improved Health

A balanced life can lead to improved physical and mental health. Prioritizing healthy habits such as exercise, sleep, and nutrition can contribute to overall well-being.

Increased Productivity

When an individual is balanced, they can approach tasks with a clear mind and focus, increasing productivity.

Greater Sense Of Fulfillment

Pursuing hobbies and spending time with loved ones can provide individuals with a sense of fulfillment and happiness that can contribute to overall satisfaction in life.

Improved Relationships

Prioritizing relationships can improve communication and foster deeper connections, leading to stronger relationships.

Personal Growth

Balancing different aspects of life can allow individuals to pursue personal growth and development. This can increase confidence, self-awareness, and a sense of purpose.

Enhanced Creativity

Taking time to engage in creative activities and pursuits can enhance creativity and innovation in other areas of life.

In conclusion, a balanced life can lead to reduced stress, improved health, increased productivity, greater fulfillment, improved relationships, personal growth, and enhanced creativity. Striving for balance in all aspects of life can contribute to overall well-being and success.

How Do Successful People Balance Work And The Rest Of Their Lives?

Successful people prioritize balancing work and the rest of their lives to achieve long-term success and fulfillment.

Here are some strategies they use:

Set Priorities

Successful people prioritize the most important tasks and activities in their lives. They clearly distinguish between work and personal life and set clear boundaries to avoid over-committing themselves.

Schedule Time For Rest And Relaxation

Successful people schedule time for relaxation in their busy lives. They take time to unwind and recharge, whether it's through meditation, exercise, or spending time with loved ones.

Outsource Tasks

Successful people understand the value of their time and delegate tasks that can be outsourced to others. This frees up time for them to focus on high-value tasks and activities.

Practice Time Management

Successful people are skilled at managing their time effectively. They prioritize tasks and eliminate distractions to maximize productivity.

Avoid Overworking

Successful people understand the importance of taking breaks and avoiding overworking. They recognize that long hours and lack of sleep can lead to burnout and reduced productivity.

Pursue Hobbies And Passions

Successful people make time for hobbies and passions outside of work. They understand that pursuing their interests can provide a sense of fulfillment and happiness, which can lead to increased motivation and productivity.

Foster Positive Relationships

Successful people prioritize positive relationships with family, friends, and colleagues. They make time to connect with others and build meaningful relationships.

In conclusion, successful people prioritize balancing work and the rest of their lives by setting priorities, scheduling rest, outsourcing tasks, practicing time management, avoiding overworking, pursuing hobbies and passions, and fostering positive relationships. By doing so, they can achieve long-term success and fulfillment while maintaining their well-being.

How Do You Have A Successful Balanced Life?

Having a successful balanced life requires intentional effort and commitment.

Here are some strategies to help achieve a balanced life:

Set Clear Goals

Start by setting clear and specific goals for all aspects of your life, including work, health, relationships, personal growth, and leisure. Write down your goals and review them regularly to stay focused and motivated.

Prioritize Self-Care

Make self-care a priority by getting enough sleep, eating a balanced diet, and engaging in regular physical activity. This will help you feel physically and mentally healthy and better equipped to manage other aspects of your life.

Practice Time Management

Effective time management is critical to achieving a balanced life. Set boundaries and prioritize your time based on your goals, avoiding distractions and procrastination.

Learn To Say No

It's important to learn to say no to commitments that don't align with your goals or that would cause excessive stress or over-commitment.

Seek Support

Build a support system of friends, family, or a therapist who can help you manage stress and provide emotional support.

Embrace Flexibility

Life can be unpredictable, so it's important to be flexible and adapt to changes in circumstances. This may mean adjusting your goals or re-prioritizing your time.

Pursue Passions

Make time for activities you enjoy, whether hobbies, travel, or spending time with loved ones. These activities can help you recharge and provide a sense of fulfillment.

Practice Gratitude

Focus on the positive aspects of your life and practice gratitude for what you have. This can help you maintain a positive mindset and reduce stress.

In conclusion, having a successful balanced life requires setting clear goals, prioritizing self-care, practicing time management, learning to say no, seeking support, embracing flexibility, pursuing passions, and practicing gratitude. By implementing these strategies, you can achieve a balanced life that promotes well-being, success, and fulfillment.

CHAPTER TWENTY-FIVE

SELF ACCEPTANCE

Self-acceptance is crucial for success as it helps individuals develop a positive self-image, build confidence, and embrace their strengths and weaknesses without judgment, leading to increased resilience and a greater ability to overcome challenges.

Why Is Self-Acceptance Important For Success?

Self-acceptance is embracing oneself, including strengths and weaknesses, without judgment or self-criticism. It is an important component of mental and emotional well-being and has been shown to play a significant role in personal and professional success.

Here are some reasons why self-acceptance is important for success:

Builds Confidence

Accepting oneself can help build self-confidence, allowing individuals to focus on their strengths and achievements rather than their flaws or shortcomings. This, in turn, can lead to tremendous success in personal and professional endeavors as individuals feel more capable and self-assured.

Reduces Stress and Anxiety

Self-acceptance can help reduce stress and anxiety by eliminating negative self-talk and self-criticism. When comfortable with themselves, individuals can better manage challenging situations, respond to stress healthily, and maintain a positive outlook.

Increases Resilience

Self-acceptance is a key component of resilience, the ability to bounce back from adversity. When individuals accept themselves, they are better equipped to handle setbacks and challenges, as they have a solid foundation of self-worth and self-esteem to draw from.

Encourages Growth and Development

Self-acceptance encourages growth and development, allowing individuals to identify areas for improvement without feeling overwhelmed or defeated. By accepting oneself as is, individuals can approach growth and development with a positive, growth-oriented mindset.

Fosters Positive Relationships

Self-acceptance can also help foster positive relationships with others, as individuals who are comfortable with themselves can better form meaningful connections and communicate effectively with others.

In conclusion, self-acceptance is important for success as it builds confidence, reduces stress and anxiety, increases resilience, encourages growth and development, and fosters positive relationships. By cultivating self-acceptance, individuals can develop the mental and emotional resilience necessary to succeed in all aspects of life.

What Is The Mindset Of Self-Acceptance?

The mindset of self-acceptance is one in which individuals can embrace themselves, including their strengths and weaknesses, without judgment or self-criticism. It is characterized by a deep sense of self-worth and an understanding that imperfection is a natural and necessary part of the human experience.

Individuals with a self-acceptance mindset can focus on their positive qualities and achievements rather than dwelling on their flaws or shortcomings. They can approach challenges with a growth-oriented mindset, viewing setbacks as opportunities for learning and growth rather than personal failures.

In addition, individuals with a mindset of self-acceptance can often maintain healthy boundaries and relationships with others. They can communicate their needs effectively and are less likely to engage in people-pleasing behaviors or compromise their values and beliefs for the sake of others.

Overall, the mindset of self-acceptance is characterized by a deep sense of self-awareness, self-compassion, and a commitment to personal growth and development. It allows individuals to navigate the ups and downs of life with greater ease and confidence and to cultivate positive, meaningful relationships with themselves and others.

Why Is Self-Acceptance Important In Leadership?

Self-acceptance is an important aspect of effective leadership. Leaders who can accept themselves for who they are, including their strengths and weaknesses, are better equipped to lead others with authenticity and compassion.

Firstly, leaders who practice self-acceptance can create a positive and inclusive work environment. Accepting their imperfections makes them less likely to judge and criticize others for their shortcomings. This creates a safe space for employees to be vulnerable and openly discuss their struggles and weaknesses, leading to more collaborative and supportive work culture.

Secondly, leaders with strong self-acceptance can make difficult decisions and take risks better. They are not held back by fear of failure or judgment from others. Instead, they can trust their intuition and decide what is best for their team and organization.

Additionally, self-acceptance allows leaders to lead with authenticity and vulnerability. Leaders can build trust and connection with their team members by being open about their strengths and weaknesses. This creates a culture of transparency and honesty, leading to more effective communication and collaboration.

Furthermore, leaders who practice self-acceptance can maintain a healthy work-life balance. By accepting their limitations and prioritizing their well-being, they are less likely to burn out or become overwhelmed by the demands of their job. This allows them to lead with a clear, focused mind and be fully present and engaged with their team.

Overall, self-acceptance is a crucial component of effective leadership. Leaders who accept themselves for who they are, including their strengths and weaknesses, are better equipped to create a positive work environment, make difficult decisions, and maintain a healthy work-life balance.

How Do You Build Self-Acceptance?

Building self-acceptance is a journey that takes time and effort. It requires a shift in mindset and a commitment to practicing self-compassion and self-love.

Here are some ways to build self-acceptance:

Practice Self-Compassion

Self-compassion involves treating yourself with kindness and understanding, just as you would treat a close friend. When you make a mistake or experience a setback, practice self-compassion by offering yourself encouragement and support.

Challenge Negative Self-Talk

Negative self-talk can be a barrier to self-acceptance. Recognizing when you're engaging in negative self-talk and challenging those thoughts is important. Ask yourself if there's evidence to support those thoughts; if not, reframe them more positively and compassionately.

Focus On Your Strengths

Instead of dwelling on your weaknesses, focus on your strengths. Celebrate your accomplishments and recognize the unique skills and talents that you bring to the table.

Practice Mindfulness

Mindfulness involves being present and non-judgmental at the moment. When you practice mindfulness, you can better observe your thoughts and emotions without getting caught up in them. This can help you develop a more accepting and compassionate attitude toward yourself.

Surround Yourself With Positive People

Surrounding yourself with people who support and encourage you can help build self-acceptance. Seek friends and mentors who uplift and remind you of your worth.

Embrace Imperfection

Accept that no one is perfect, including yourself. Embracing imperfection can help you overcome unrealistic expectations and cultivate a more compassionate attitude toward yourself.

Seek Help When Needed

If you're struggling to build self-acceptance, don't be afraid to seek help. Talk to a therapist or counselor who can help you work through any underlying issues or negative thought patterns that may hold you back.

Remember, building self-acceptance is a journey that takes time and effort. But by practicing self-compassion, challenging negative self-talk, focusing on your strengths, practicing mindfulness, surrounding yourself with positive people, embracing imperfection, and seeking help, you can cultivate a more accepting and compassionate attitude towards yourself.

CHAPTER TWENTY-SIX

EMBRACE POSSIBILITIES

Embracing new ideas and possibilities is essential for success because it allows individuals to stay innovative, adaptable, and open-minded to new opportunities and growth potential. Without this willingness to explore new ideas, individuals can become stagnant and miss out on valuable personal and professional development opportunities.

Why Is It Important To Embrace New Ideas?

Embracing new ideas is vital for personal and professional growth. It enables us to evolve, develop, and advance in our careers and personal lives.

Here are some reasons why it's important to embrace new ideas:

Innovation

New ideas often lead to innovation. By embracing new ideas, we can explore new ways of doing things, discover new technologies, and create new solutions to problems. This can lead to significant breakthroughs that positively impact our personal and professional lives.

Adaptability

Embracing new ideas helps us become more adaptable. When we're open to new ideas, we can adapt to changes in our environment and respond more effectively to challenges. This ability to adapt is crucial in today's fast-paced and ever-changing world.

Growth

Embracing new ideas can help us grow as individuals. When we're open to new ideas, we're more likely to take risks and step outside our comfort zones. This can lead to personal and professional growth as we learn new skills and develop new perspectives.

Creativity

New ideas often spark creativity. When we're open to new ideas, we're more likely to think creatively and develop innovative solutions to problems. This can lead to new opportunities and possibilities that we may not have otherwise considered.

Collaboration

Embracing new ideas fosters collaboration. When we're open to new ideas, we're more likely to collaborate, share ideas, and learn from one another. This can lead to stronger relationships and more productive teams.

In conclusion, embracing new ideas is essential for personal and professional growth. It helps us become more innovative, adaptable, and creative and fosters collaboration and growth. By embracing new ideas, we can unlock our full potential and achieve success in all areas of our lives.

How To Open Your Mind To New Ideas And Possibilities?

Opening your mind to new ideas and possibilities is essential for personal and professional growth.

Here are some tips to help you cultivate an open mind:

Be Curious

Start by being curious about the world around you. Ask questions, seek out new experiences, and be open to learning new things.

Challenge Your Beliefs

Examine your beliefs and opinions and be open to changing them. Be willing to consider new perspectives and viewpoints.

Embrace Diversity

Seek out diverse experiences and people. Surround yourself with people who have different backgrounds, cultures, and experiences from your own.

Practice Mindfulness

Practice being present at the moment and paying attention to your thoughts and feelings. This can help you become more aware of your biases and open to new ideas.

Read And Learn

Read books, articles, and other materials that challenge your thinking and expose you to new ideas and perspectives.

Try New Things

Be willing to step outside your comfort zone and try new things. This can be as simple as trying a new food or as complex as taking on a new project at work.

Embrace Failure

Recognize that failure is a natural part of the learning process. Embrace, learn from, and use it to fuel your growth and development.

Surround Yourself With Diverse Perspectives

Engage in conversations with people who have different viewpoints and perspectives than your own. This can help you see things from a different angle and learn new ways of thinking.

Practice Empathy

Try to understand the perspectives of others and put yourself in their shoes. This can help you become more open-minded and compassionate.

In conclusion, opening your mind to new ideas and possibilities is crucial for personal and professional growth. By being curious, challenging your beliefs, embracing diversity, practicing mindfulness, reading, learning, trying new things, embracing failure, surrounding yourself with diverse perspectives, and practicing empathy, you can cultivate an open mind and unlock your full potential.

Why Is Innovation Important For Business Success?

Innovation is essential for business success in today's rapidly changing marketplace.

Here are some reasons why:

Competitive Advantage

Innovation allows businesses to differentiate themselves from competitors by offering unique products, services, and experiences.

Increased Efficiency And Productivity

Innovation can lead to the development of new technologies, processes, and systems that increase efficiency and productivity.

Improved Customer Satisfaction

Innovation can result in the creation of products and services that better meet the needs and wants of customers, leading to higher levels of customer satisfaction and loyalty.

Reduced Costs

Innovation can lead to cost savings by developing new technologies and processes that streamline operations and reduce waste.

New Revenue Streams

Innovation can create new opportunities for revenue growth by opening up new markets or expanding existing ones.

Future-Proofing

Innovation helps businesses stay ahead of the curve by anticipating and adapting to changes in the market and technology landscape.

Attract And Retain Talent

Businesses prioritizing innovation are more attractive to top talent looking for opportunities to work on cutting-edge projects and technologies.

Social And Environmental Impact

Innovation can lead to the development of products and services that have a positive social or environmental impact, which can enhance a company's reputation and brand value.

In conclusion, to stay ahead in today's rapidly changing marketplace, businesses must prioritize innovation and invest in developing new technologies, products, and services.

How To Come Up With Innovative Ideas At Work?

Coming up with innovative ideas can be challenging, but there are several strategies you can use to stimulate creativity and generate new ideas at work.

Here are some tips:

Ask Questions

Ask open-ended questions to encourage discussion and brainstorming. For example, "What if we could completely redesign this product/service from scratch?" or "How can we solve this problem in a completely different way?"

Collaborate

Collaborate with colleagues from different departments or backgrounds to bring new perspectives and ideas to the table. Encourage open communication and a culture of experimentation and risk-taking.

Research

Keep up-to-date with the latest trends and technologies in your industry by attending conferences, reading industry publications, and networking with other professionals. This can help you identify opportunities for innovation and inspire new ideas.

Embrace Failure

Encourage a culture where failure is seen as a learning opportunity rather than a negative outcome. Allow yourself and your team to take risks and experiment with new ideas, even if they don't always work out.

Take Breaks

Give your brain a break by taking regular breaks and engaging in activities that help to relax and recharge your mind. This can include taking a walk, meditating, or taking a few deep breaths.

Encourage Creativity

Create a workspace that encourages creativity and inspiration, such as a collaborative meeting room or a space with bright colors and comfortable seating.

Be Customer-Focused

Keep your customers' needs and preferences at the forefront of your mind when generating new ideas. Ask for feedback and involve them in the ideation process to ensure that your ideas are relevant and valuable to them.

In conclusion, coming up with innovative ideas at work requires a combination of creativity, collaboration, research, experimentation, and a customer-focused mindset. Implementing these strategies stimulates creativity and generates new ideas to drive business success and growth.

CHAPTER TWENTY-SEVEN

TRUST INTUITION

Sharpening your intuition can be an important tool for success, as it can help you make better decisions and identify opportunities that might otherwise be missed. By tuning into your intuition, you can gain greater clarity and confidence in your choices.

What Is Intuition, And Why Is It Important?

Intuition is an innate sense of knowing that comes from within rather than external factors such as logic or reason. It is often described as a gut feeling, a hunch, or an instinctive response to a situation or decision. While intuition can be difficult to define or measure, it can play an important role in our lives and decision-making processes.

Intuition is important for several reasons. Firstly, it can help us make better decisions. When we listen to our intuition, we tap into our subconscious knowledge and experiences, which can help us see things more clearly and make choices aligned with our values and goals. Intuition can also alert us to potential risks or dangers that may not be immediately apparent, helping us avoid adverse outcomes.

Secondly, intuition can help us identify opportunities that might otherwise be missed. By tuning into our intuition, we may notice patterns or connections that we would not have seen otherwise, leading us to innovative solutions or new paths. In this way, intuition can be a powerful tool for creativity and innovation.

Finally, intuition can help us connect with others on a deeper level. When we trust our intuition and listen to our inner voice, we become more authentic and present in our interactions with others. This can lead to more meaningful relationships, as we can communicate more effectively and empathetically.

While intuition can be a valuable resource, it is important to note that it should not be relied upon exclusively. Balancing our intuitive responses with rational thought and analysis is important to make well-informed decisions. By cultivating our intuition and learning to trust it, we can develop a more holistic approach to decision-making and problem-solving, leading to greater success and fulfillment in our lives.

How To Sharpen Your Intuition For Success?

Intuition is a skill that can be developed and strengthened over time with practice. Here are some tips on how to sharpen your intuition for success:

Practice Mindfulness

Mindfulness meditation can help you quiet your mind and tune in to your intuition. You can better distinguish between your intuition and other mental chatter when you are more aware of your thoughts and feelings.

Pay Attention To Your Physical Sensations

Often, our intuition manifests as a physical sensation in our bodies, such as a tightness in our chest or a feeling of lightness. By paying attention to these sensations, we can better understand our intuition and use it to guide us.

Keep A Journal

Writing down your thoughts and feelings can help you track patterns and identify when your intuition is speaking to you. Over time, you may notice themes or insights that can help you make better decisions.

Practice Decision-Making

Making small decisions based on intuition can help you build confidence in your inner voice. Start with low-risk decisions, such as what to wear or eat, and work your way up to bigger decisions.

Seek Out New Experiences

Trying new things can help you expand your perspective and open yourself to new insights and ideas. This can help you develop a more intuitive approach to problem-solving.

Trust Yourself

One of the most important aspects of developing intuition is learning to trust yourself. Trust that your inner voice is guiding you toward what is best for you, even if it doesn't always make logical sense.

By practicing these techniques and learning to trust your intuition, you can sharpen your intuitive skills and use them to make better decisions and achieve greater success in your personal and professional life.

How To Stop Overthinking And Start Trusting Your Gut?

Overthinking can cause stress and anxiety and prevent you from making decisions based on your intuition.

Here are some tips on how to stop overthinking and start trusting your gut:

Identify Your Triggers

Identify the situations that trigger overthinking for you. Once you have identified your triggers, you can take steps to avoid or manage them.

Practice Mindfulness

Mindfulness can help you to be more present at the moment and stop your mind from wandering. This can help you to tune into your intuition and make better decisions.

Trust Yourself

Trust that you can make good decisions based on your intuition. Have confidence in yourself and your abilities.

Stop Seeking Approval

Stop seeking approval from others and trust your judgment. This can be challenging, but it's important to remember that you know yourself best.

Take Action

Overthinking can paralyze you and prevent you from taking action. Make a decision and take action, even if it's a small step. This can help you build momentum and gain confidence in your decision-making ability.

Reflect On Past Experiences

Reflect on past experiences where you followed your intuition, and it led to a positive outcome. This can give you the confidence to trust your intuition in future decision-making.

Don't Second-Guess Yourself

Once you have made a decision based on your intuition, don't second-guess yourself. Trust that you made the best decision based on the information you had at the time.

Remember that trusting your gut takes practice, and it's important to be patient and kind to yourself as you learn to rely on your intuition more. By stopping overthinking and trusting your gut, you can make better decisions and live a more fulfilling life.

CHAPTER TWENTY-EIGHT

READER

Reading is crucial to success as it can help expand knowledge, enhance critical thinking and problem-solving skills, and improve communication. Successful people often attribute their achievements to being avid readers and lifelong learners.

Why Are Readers More Successful?

Reading is a key factor in achieving success in various areas of life. Successful people are often avid readers who recognize the benefits of regularly consuming written material.

Here are some reasons why readers are more successful:

Expanding Knowledge

Reading is an excellent way to acquire new information and expand one's knowledge base. Reading books, articles, and other written material allows individuals to gain insights into different fields and disciplines, enabling them to think creatively and solve problems more effectively.

Developing Critical Thinking Skills

Reading helps develop critical thinking skills by challenging readers to analyze, evaluate, and interpret information. It helps individuals develop a deeper understanding of complex issues and situations, enabling them to make better decisions in various aspects of life.

Enhancing Communication Abilities

Reading allows individuals to learn new vocabulary and language structures, which helps improve their communication abilities. Reading also exposes readers to different writing styles, enabling them to improve their writing skills and become more effective communicators.

Increasing Empathy And Emotional Intelligence

Reading can help individuals develop empathy and emotional intelligence by exposing them to different perspectives and experiences. It allows readers to understand human emotions and behavior better, enabling them to connect more effectively with others.

Reducing Stress

Reading has been shown to have a calming effect on the mind, reducing stress and anxiety. It can help individuals relax and unwind, enabling them to approach challenges with a clear and focused mindset.

Overall, reading is a powerful tool that can help individuals achieve success in various areas of life. By regularly reading and expanding their knowledge base, individuals can develop the skills and abilities needed to reach their goals and achieve their full potential.

How Does Reading Make You More Intelligent?

Reading is an essential activity that stimulates the brain and promotes cognitive development. Studies have shown that reading can increase intelligence by improving vocabulary, reasoning skills, and general knowledge. Reading also exercises the brain, making it more efficient in processing information and retaining memory.

Through reading, individuals are exposed to new ideas, perspectives, and information that can expand their understanding of the world. This exposure to new information helps to improve critical thinking skills and encourages creative problem-solving. Reading can also improve language skills, including spelling, grammar, and writing, significantly impacting academic and professional success.

Additionally, reading can help to reduce stress and promote mental health. Engaging in a good book can provide an escape from the pressures of daily life and promote relaxation. Reading can also help increase empathy and understanding of others, leading to improved social skills and stronger interpersonal relationships.

It's important to make it a regular habit to reap the benefits of reading. Setting aside time each day or each week for reading can help to make it a priority in your life. Choosing books that align with your interests and goals can also help to keep you engaged and motivated to continue reading. It's also helpful to have a variety of reading materials available, including books, articles, and blogs, to keep things interesting and engaging.

In conclusion, reading is a powerful tool for personal and professional growth. It can increase intelligence, improve language skills, promote mental health, and expand our understanding of the world. By making reading a regular habit, we can cultivate a love for learning and continue to grow and develop throughout our lives.

Why Is Reading Important In Professional Development?

Reading is essential to professional development because it allows individuals to expand their knowledge and stay up-to-date on industry trends. By reading relevant books, articles, and other materials, professionals can gain new perspectives and insights to help them make better decisions and perform their jobs more effectively.

One of the main benefits of reading in professional development is that it gives individuals access to a wealth of information and ideas. Whether trying to learn a new skill or stay current on the latest industry trends, reading can help you acquire the knowledge and expertise you need to succeed. It can also help you stay up-to-date on new technologies, techniques, and best practices to improve your performance and productivity.

Reading also allows individuals to broaden their perspectives and think more critically about their work. Professionals can better understand their industry and its challenges by exposing themselves to diverse viewpoints and ideas. This can help them identify new opportunities and solutions they may not have considered before.

Moreover, reading can also enhance communication skills. By reading different genres, professionals can improve their vocabulary, writing skills, and ability to articulate ideas effectively. This can be especially important in industries where effective communication is critical, such as marketing, sales, or management.

In addition, reading can help professionals to stay motivated and inspired. Reading about the successes and challenges of others in their field can provide encouragement and inspiration, helping individuals to push themselves further and achieve their goals. Furthermore, reading can be a source of relaxation and stress relief, improving mental health and well-being.

Overall, reading is an important component of professional development. It can broaden knowledge, improve communication skills, foster critical thinking, and inspire individuals to achieve their goals. By dedicating time to reading, professionals can continue to grow and thrive in their careers.

How To Cultivate A Lifetime Reading Habit?

Cultivating a lifetime reading habit can be a great way to gain knowledge and expand one's worldview.

Here are a few tips to help you develop this habit:

Make Reading A Priority

Set aside a specific time each day for reading, even if it's just 10-15 minutes. This will help you make reading a habit and ensure that you stick to it.

Choose Books That Interest You

Read books that pique your curiosity or capture your attention, whether a novel or a non-fiction book on a subject you are passionate about. This will make reading more enjoyable and engaging.

Create A Reading List

Make a list of books you want to read and add to it regularly. This will give you a sense of purpose and direction and make it easier to choose your next book.

Create A Comfortable Reading Space

Set up a comfortable reading space with good lighting, a comfortable chair, and minimal distractions. This will help you to focus and make reading a relaxing and enjoyable experience.

Join A Book Club

Joining a book club or online reading community can help you to stay motivated and engaged. It also provides an opportunity to discuss books with others, which can deepen your understanding and appreciation of what you have read.

By following these tips, you can cultivate a lifetime reading habit that will enhance your knowledge, creativity, and personal growth.

CHAPTER TWENTY-NINE

ACTION ORIENTED

Action-oriented is important because success comes from consistent action toward one's goals and aspirations. Those who take action are likelier to succeed than those who dream or plan without action.

What Does It Mean To Be Action-Oriented?

Being action-oriented means an individual has a proactive mindset, takes the initiative, and is driven to act toward their goals and objectives. It involves being biased towards action rather than just thinking or talking about things. Action-oriented individuals are motivated to identify the necessary steps to achieve their goals and take action toward them, even in the face of obstacles or setbacks.

Being action-oriented also means having a sense of urgency to get things done and being willing to learn and adapt. Rather than being paralyzed by fear or indecision, action-oriented individuals focus on making progress, even if it means taking small steps at a time. They also recognize the importance of taking calculated risks and embracing failure as a natural part of the learning process.

Overall, being action-oriented is a crucial trait of successful individuals, as it allows them to turn their goals and aspirations into tangible results through consistent effort and focused action.

Why Is It Important To Be Action-Oriented?

Action-oriented means having a mindset focused on taking action and progressing toward one's goals. It involves prioritizing action over mere planning or thinking. There are several reasons why being action-oriented is important for success.

Firstly, taking action is essential for achieving one's goals. Without action, ideas and plans are merely fantasies. Taking action moves one closer to their goal and helps to build momentum. As progress is made, motivation increases, leading to even more action and progress.

Secondly, being action-oriented builds resilience and adaptability. When one takes action, they gain experience and learn from their mistakes. This helps build resilience and adaptability as they become more comfortable taking risks and making necessary adjustments.

Lastly, being action-oriented sets one apart from others. Ideas and plans are plentiful in many cases, but those who take action and implement their ideas are few. Being action-oriented makes one stand out and differentiate themselves from their competitors.

It is important to prioritize action over perfection to be action-oriented. Instead of waiting for the perfect plan or idea, one should take action and make adjustments along the way. It is also important to focus on progress over outcomes. Progress, no matter how small, is still progress and can help build momentum toward achieving one's goals.

In addition, it is important to set clear goals and develop an action plan to achieve them. Break down the goals into smaller, actionable steps that can be achieved within a specific timeframe. This helps to make the goals more achievable and helps to keep one focused on taking action.

Finally, it is important to hold oneself accountable for taking action. This can involve seeking feedback from others, tracking progress, and celebrating successes. By holding oneself accountable, one is more likely to stay motivated and focused on taking action toward achieving their goals.

How To Strengthen Your Action-Orientation Ability?

Action orientation refers to the ability to take action toward achieving one's goals and objectives. It involves being proactive, decisive, and taking responsibility for one's actions. Developing and strengthening this ability is crucial for achieving success in both personal and professional life.

Here are some tips on how to strengthen your action-orientation ability:

Set Clear Goals

The first step in becoming action-oriented is to define your goals. Setting clear and specific goals helps to provide direction and focus. Write down your goals, break them into smaller achievable steps, and set deadlines.

Prioritize Tasks

Prioritizing tasks helps to ensure that the most important tasks are completed first. Learning how to distinguish between urgent and important tasks and allocate time accordingly is essential.

Take Calculated Risks

Taking calculated risks is an essential part of being action-oriented. It involves stepping out of your comfort zone and taking on new challenges. It is essential to weigh the pros and cons of any decision before taking action.

Develop A Positive Mindset

Developing a positive mindset is critical to becoming action-oriented. Believe in yourself and your ability to succeed. Focus on solutions rather than problems, and learn from mistakes instead of dwelling on them.

Take Action

The most crucial step in becoming action-oriented is to take action. Avoid procrastination and take action toward achieving your goals. Break down larger tasks into smaller ones and take small steps daily to make progress.

Learn To Adapt

Flexibility and adaptability are crucial in today's fast-paced world. Learn to adjust your approach and change course when necessary. Stay open-minded and be willing to learn from others.

Surround Yourself With Action-Oriented People

Surrounding yourself with action-oriented people can help to motivate and inspire you. Seek out mentors or colleagues who share similar goals and values.

In conclusion, becoming action-oriented is an essential skill that can be developed and strengthened over time. By setting clear goals, prioritizing tasks, taking calculated risks, developing a positive mindset, taking action, learning to adapt, and surrounding yourself with action-oriented people, you can enhance your ability to achieve your goals and succeed in both your personal and professional life.

CHAPTER THIRTY

PREPARED

Preparation is crucial to achieving your goals as it helps you anticipate challenges, develop a plan of action, and build confidence in your abilities to succeed. Without proper preparation, you may find yourself ill-equipped to overcome obstacles or take advantage of opportunities when they arise.

Why Is Preparation Important To Success?

Preparation is the key to success. It is the process of planning, organizing, and practicing in advance for an upcoming task or event. Preparation can significantly increase the chances of success in any endeavor, whether a job interview, a sports game, a public speaking engagement, or an academic exam.

Here, we will discuss why preparation is important to success and how it can help individuals achieve their goals.

Firstly, preparation helps individuals to identify their strengths and weaknesses. Individuals can assess their knowledge, skills, and abilities through preparation and determine improvement areas. This self-awareness is critical to success, as it allows individuals to focus on areas that require attention and develop strategies to overcome their weaknesses.

Secondly, preparation provides individuals with a sense of confidence and control. When well-prepared, individuals feel more confident and in control of the situation. This confidence translates into better performance, as individuals are less likely to be distracted by self-doubt or anxiety. Moreover, well-prepared individuals are more likely to adapt to unexpected challenges or obstacles, as they have already considered various scenarios and developed contingency plans.

Thirdly, preparation saves time and reduces stress. Individuals can complete tasks more efficiently and with less stress when preparing in advance. For example, a student who has studied for an exam in advance is less likely to feel overwhelmed or panicked during the actual exam. Similarly, a business professional prepared for a meeting in advance is more likely to stay on track and accomplish their objectives without wasting time or energy.

In conclusion, preparation is essential to success. It allows individuals to identify their strengths and weaknesses, gain confidence and control, save time, and reduce stress. Individuals can achieve their goals and succeed in any endeavor by investing time and effort in preparation. Therefore, it is essential to make preparation a habit and a priority in all aspects of life.

How Does Preparation Help You Reach Your Goals?

Preparation is an essential element in achieving your goals. It is the process of planning, organizing, and practicing in advance to ensure success. Whether you have personal, academic, or professional goals, preparation can help you reach them efficiently and effectively.

Here, we will explore how preparation helps you reach your goals.

Firstly, preparation allows you to clarify your goals. When you take the time to plan and organize, you can define your goals and objectives in detail. This clarity helps you focus on your goals and create a clear path. You can break down your goals into smaller, more manageable tasks, making them less daunting and more achievable.

Secondly, preparation helps you build momentum. You can start taking steps toward your goals when you have a clear action plan. The more progress you make, the more motivated you become, and the easier it becomes to keep going. By preparing well, you can create a sense of momentum that drives you forward toward your objectives.

Thirdly, preparation helps you anticipate and overcome obstacles. When you prepare, you can identify potential obstacles on your path to success. You can then develop strategies to overcome them, reducing these obstacles' impact on your progress. This preparation can help you stay on track and focused on your goals.

Fourthly, preparation helps you build confidence. When you have a clear plan of action and have practiced in advance, you feel more confident about your ability to succeed. This confidence translates into better performance, as you are less likely to be distracted by self-doubt or anxiety. You can approach your goals with a positive mindset, which can help you achieve better results.

In conclusion, preparation is a critical element in reaching your goals. It helps you clarify your goals, build momentum, anticipate and overcome obstacles, and build confidence. Investing time and effort in preparation can increase your chances of success and help you achieve your goals more efficiently and effectively. Therefore, it is essential to make preparation a habit and a priority in all aspects of life.

Why Should You Be Prepared At Work?

Being prepared at work is crucial for success, efficiency, and productivity. Preparation means being ready for any task or challenge that comes your way and having the necessary skills and knowledge to handle it. Being prepared at work can help you in many ways, whether you are a new employee or a seasoned professional.

Firstly, being prepared at work helps you perform better. When you are well-prepared, you can complete tasks more efficiently and effectively. You are less likely to make mistakes or miss important details, which can affect the quality of your work. This, in turn, helps you build a positive reputation at work and increases your chances of advancement.

Secondly, being prepared at work reduces stress. When well-prepared, you are less likely to feel overwhelmed or anxious about your workload. You have a plan in place, and you know how to handle any challenges that come your way. This sense of control can reduce your stress levels and make work more enjoyable.

Thirdly, being prepared at work demonstrates your professionalism. Employers value well-prepared employees, as it shows that they take their work seriously and are committed to delivering high-quality results. This can lead to greater respect from your colleagues and may even increase opportunities and promotions.

Fourthly, being prepared at work allows you to be more proactive. When well-prepared, you can anticipate potential problems or issues and develop strategies to address them. This proactive approach can help you identify opportunities for improvement and make suggestions for changes that can benefit your team or organization.

In conclusion, being prepared at work is essential for success, efficiency, and productivity. It helps you perform better, reduces stress, demonstrates professionalism, and allows you to be more proactive. Investing time and effort in preparation can increase your chances of success and build a positive reputation at work. Therefore, it is essential to make preparation a habit and a priority in your work life.

How Do You Prepare To Achieve Your Goals?

Achieving your goals requires careful planning and preparation. Preparation involves taking the necessary steps to ensure you have the skills, resources, and mindset to achieve your goals.

Firstly, identify your goals. You cannot prepare for something if you don't know what it is. Be specific and clear about what you want to achieve. Write down your goals and break them into smaller, more manageable tasks. This will help you stay organized and focused on what needs to be done.

Secondly, research and gather information. Once you have identified your goals, gather as much information as possible. This can include researching online, reading books or articles, attending workshops, or talking to experts in the field. The more information you have, the better prepared you will be to achieve your goals.

Thirdly, develop a plan. Once you clearly understand what you want to achieve and the information you need, develop an action plan. Create a timeline and set deadlines for each task. This will help you stay on track and ensure that you are making progress toward your goals.

Fourthly, acquire the necessary skills and resources. Identify the skills and resources you need to achieve your goals. This may involve taking courses, seeking mentorship, or investing in equipment or technology. Ensure that you have the necessary resources at your disposal before you begin.

Fifthly, practice and review. Practice is essential to achieving your goals. Practice and review your progress regularly to ensure that you are on track. This will also help you identify areas where you need to improve or adjust your plan.

In conclusion, preparing to achieve your goals involves identifying your goals, researching and gathering information, developing a plan, acquiring necessary skills and resources, and practicing and reviewing regularly. By following these steps, you can increase your chances of success and achieve your goals more efficiently and effectively. Remember, preparation is key to success.

CHAPTER THIRTY-ONE

BRAVE

Taking risks is important because it allows you to step out of your comfort zone and experience personal and professional growth. It can lead to new opportunities and successes you may have never thought possible.

How Does Courage Lead To Success?

Courage is the ability to take action in the face of fear and uncertainty. It is an essential quality that can lead to success in all areas of life, including personal, professional, and social.

Let's discuss how courage leads to success.

Firstly, courage allows you to take risks. Success often involves taking risks and stepping out of your comfort zone. Having the courage to take those risks can lead to new opportunities and experiences that can contribute to your success.

Secondly, courage helps you overcome obstacles. Success is not always a straight path, and obstacles will arise. Having the courage to face those obstacles head-on can help you overcome them and continue on your path to success.

Thirdly, courage fosters resilience. Success requires persistence and resilience, and courage is a key component. It allows you to bounce back from setbacks and failures and keep moving toward your goals.

Fourthly, courage inspires others. When you demonstrate courage, you inspire others to do the same. It can create a positive environment of growth and success.

In conclusion, courage is an essential quality that can lead to success in all areas of life. It allows you to take risks, overcome obstacles, foster resilience, and inspire others. By cultivating courage, you can increase your chances of success and create a fulfilling and meaningful life.

What Is The Importance Of Taking Risks?

Taking risks is essential for personal and professional growth. It involves stepping out of your comfort zone and facing uncertainty to pursue a goal or opportunity.

Now, we will discuss the importance of taking risks.

Firstly, taking risks helps you overcome fear. Fear can be a powerful inhibitor, holding us back from pursuing our dreams or taking on new challenges. By taking risks, we confront our fears and build resilience, which can help us to overcome future challenges.

Secondly, taking risks leads to new opportunities. Opportunities often come disguised as risks and taking a chance can lead to unexpected, positive outcomes. You may discover new talents or interests, meet new people, or find success in unexpected ways.

Thirdly, taking risks builds confidence. When you take a risk and succeed, it can boost your self-confidence and self-esteem. This can create a positive cycle of taking on new challenges and achieving more significant successes.

Fourthly, taking risks fosters innovation. Innovation often requires taking risks and trying new things. Without taking risks, progress and innovation can stagnate. Taking risks can spark creativity and develop new ideas and approaches.

Fifthly, taking risks helps you learn from failure. Failure is an inevitable part of life, but it can be an opportunity for growth and learning. By taking risks and experiencing failure, you can learn from your mistakes, make necessary adjustments, and become better equipped to handle future challenges.

In conclusion, taking risks is essential for personal and professional growth. It helps you overcome fear, leads to new opportunities, builds confidence, fosters innovation, and helps you learn from failure. Taking calculated risks and being open to new experiences can increase your chances of success and create a more fulfilling life.

How Does Taking Risks Open New Opportunities?

Taking risks can open up new opportunities by:

Expanding Your Horizons

By taking risks, you step outside your comfort zone and explore new experiences and opportunities you may have never considered.

Building New Skills

Taking risks often involves learning new skills or developing existing ones. This can lead to new opportunities in areas you may have never considered before.

Networking

Taking risks can also lead to new networking opportunities. Meeting new people can open doors to opportunities and connections that benefit your personal and professional growth.

Creating New Pathways

Taking risks can create new pathways for success you may have never thought possible. It can open new industries, careers, and personal and professional growth avenues.

Overcoming Fear

Fear is often what holds us back from pursuing new opportunities. We build resilience and become better equipped to handle future challenges by taking risks and facing our fears.

Improving Decision-Making Skills

Taking risks requires making decisions, often with limited information. This can improve your decision-making skills, making you more effective personally and professionally.

Inspiring Others

When you take risks, you inspire others to do the same. This can create a positive environment of growth and learning, leading to new opportunities for all involved.

Enhancing Creativity

Taking risks can also enhance creativity. It encourages you to think outside the box and develop new solutions and approaches to problems.

Building Confidence

Taking risks and achieving success can boost your confidence and self-esteem. This can create a positive cycle of taking on new challenges and achieving greater success.

In conclusion, taking risks opens up new opportunities by expanding your horizons, building new skills, networking, creating new pathways, overcoming fear, improving decision-making skills, inspiring others, enhancing creativity, and building confidence. Taking calculated risks and being open to new experiences can increase your chances of success and create a more fulfilling life.

Why Do Successful Entrepreneurs Need To Be Calculated Risk-Takers?

Successful entrepreneurs need to be calculated risk-takers because taking risks is an inherent part of entrepreneurship. However, they cannot afford to take reckless risks as it could lead to significant losses and jeopardize their business.

Calculated risk-taking involves assessing a particular decision's potential risks and rewards, weighing the potential outcomes, and making an informed decision based on the available information. Entrepreneurs must be able to evaluate risks and opportunities quickly and make strategic decisions based on their findings.

Being a calculated risk-taker requires an entrepreneur to be knowledgeable, prepared, and flexible. They must deeply understand their market, competition, and customers to make informed decisions. They also need to have contingency plans in place to mitigate any potential risks that may arise.

Successful entrepreneurs also need to be able to adapt quickly to changing circumstances. They must be able to pivot and adjust their strategies to respond to market conditions and take advantage of new opportunities.

In conclusion, calculated risk-taking is an essential trait for successful entrepreneurs. It involves assessing potential risks and rewards, making informed decisions, and being knowledgeable, prepared, and flexible. Entrepreneurs who take calculated risks and adapt quickly to changing circumstances have a better chance of success in their businesses.

How To Take Calculated Risks In Business?

Taking calculated risks in business involves making informed decisions based on a thorough assessment of potential risks and rewards.

Here are some tips on how to take calculated risks in business:

Conduct Thorough Research

Before making any significant business decision, conduct thorough research on the market, competition, and potential customers. This will help you better understand the potential risks and rewards associated with the decision.

Define Your Goals

Clearly define your goals and objectives before making any decision. This will help you evaluate whether a particular decision aligns with your business objectives and will help you avoid making impulsive decisions.

Weigh The Potential Outcomes

Analyze the potential outcomes of the decision you are considering. Consider the best-case scenario, worst-case scenario, and everything in between. This will help you determine whether the potential rewards outweigh the potential risks.

Create Contingency Plans

Be prepared for any potential risks that may arise by creating contingency plans. This will help you minimize potential losses and respond quickly to unexpected situations.

Seek Input From Trusted Advisors

Seek input from trusted advisors, such as business partners, mentors, or industry experts. This will help you gain different perspectives and identify potential blind spots in your decision-making process.

Test The Waters

Before making a significant investment or committing to a major decision, test the waters by conducting a small-scale trial or pilot. This will help you evaluate the potential success of the decision on a smaller scale before investing significant resources.

Learn From Past Mistakes

Reflect on past business decisions and identify areas where you could have made better choices. Use these insights to inform your decision-making process moving forward.

In conclusion, taking calculated risks in business involves conducting thorough research, defining goals, weighing potential outcomes, creating contingency plans, seeking input from trusted advisors, testing the waters, and learning from past mistakes. By taking calculated risks, entrepreneurs can maximize their chances of success and achieve their business objectives.

How To Be More Courageous In The Workplace?

Being more courageous in the workplace can help individuals take on new challenges and achieve their career goals.

Here are some tips on how to be more courageous in the workplace:

Identify Your Fears

Identify what is holding you back and keeping you from being courageous. It could be fear of failure, rejection, or criticism. Once you identify your fears, you can work on overcoming them.

Set Goals

Set clear and achievable goals for yourself. This will give you a clear sense of direction and purpose and help you stay motivated and focused.

Take Small Steps

Start by taking small steps outside your comfort zone. This could be volunteering for a new project or speaking up in a meeting. As you become more comfortable taking small risks, you can gradually take on bigger challenges.

Practice Self-Care

Taking care of your physical and emotional well-being can help boost your confidence and resilience, making it easier to be courageous in the workplace.

Surround Yourself With Support

Surround yourself with colleagues, mentors, and friends who support and encourage you. Having a strong support system can help you stay motivated and confident.

Learn From Failures

Don't be afraid of failure. Instead, use it as an opportunity to learn and grow. By reframing failure as a learning experience, you can build resilience and become more courageous in the workplace.

In conclusion, being more courageous in the workplace requires identifying your fears, setting goals, taking small steps, practicing self-care, surrounding yourself with support, and learning from failures. Individuals can build confidence and resilience and ultimately achieve their career goals by taking these steps.

Develop The Traits And Qualities Of Highly Successful People

Throughout this book, I explored the various traits and qualities of highly successful people. From persistence and determination to creativity and adaptability, these characteristics are essential for achieving success in any area of life. I hope this book has provided valuable insights and inspiration to develop these qualities within yourself.

Knowing where you currently stand regarding the traits and qualities discussed in this book is important to become more successful. While knowing about these traits and qualities is important, putting them into action is even more crucial.

I want to express my gratitude to the people who have contributed to the creation of this book. This includes my wife and other supporters who have provided feedback, encouragement, and assistance.

Thank you for reading this book, and I wish you all the best on your journey toward success!

Printed by Libri Plureos GmbH in Hamburg,
Germany